The Choice of
and the
to the Religions State
by
St Alphonsus M Liguori

St Athanasius Press
All Rights Reserved 2014

ISBN-13: 978-1499237320

ISBN-10: 1499237324

St Athanasius Press
133 Slazing Rd
Potosi, WI 53820
melwaller@gmail.com
(email is the best way to reach us)
www.stathanasiuspress.com

Specializing in Reprinting Catholic Classics

Check out our other Titles

at the end of the book!

CONTENTS

The Choice of a State of Life, and the Vocation to the Religions State.

COUNSELS CONCERNING A RELIGIOUS VOCATION.

I.

We ought to conform to the Designs of God in the Choice of a State of Life, whatever it may be.

It is evident that our eternal salvation depends principally upon the choice of our state of life. Father Granada calls this choice the chief wheel of our whole life. Hence, as when in a clock the chief wheel is deranged, the whole clock is also deranged, so in the order of our salvation, if we make a mistake as to the state to which we are called, our whole life, as St. Gregory Nazianzen says, will be an error.

If, then, in the choice of a state of life, we wish to secure our eternal salvation, we must embrace that to which God calls us, in which only God prepares for us the efficacious means necessary to our salvation. For, as St Cyprian says: "The grace of the Holy Spirit is given according to the order of God, and not according to our own will;" and therefore St. Paul writes, Every one hath his proper gift from God." That is, as Cornelius a Lapide explains it, God gives to everyone his vocation, and chooses the state in which he wills him to be saved. And this is the order of predestination described by the same apostle: Whom he predestinated, them he also called; and whom he called, them he also justified, . . . and them he also glorified.

We must remark that in the world this doctrine of the voca-

6

tion is not much studied by some persons. They think it to be all the same, whether they live in the state to which God calls them, or in that which they choose of their own inclination, and therefore so many live a bad life and damn themselves.

But it is certain that this is the principal point with regard to the acquisition of eternal life. He who disturbs this order and breaks this chain of salvation will not be saved. With all his labors and with all the good he may do, St. Augustine will tell him, "Thou runnest well, but out of the way," that is, out of the way in which God has called you to walk for attaining to salvation. The Lord does not accept the sacrifices offered up to him from our own inclination, But to Cain and his offerings he had no respect. Rather he threatens with great chastisement those who, when he calls them, turn their backs on him in order to follow the whims of their own caprice. Woe to you apostate children, he says through Isaias, that you would take counsel and not from me, and would begin a web and not by my spirit.

II.

The Vocation to the Religious State. How Important it is to follow it promptly.

1. MISERY TO WHICH ONE EXPOSES ONE'S SELF BY NOT CORRESPONDING TO IT.

The divine call to a more perfect life is undoubtedly a special grace, and a very great one, which God does not give to all; hence he has much reason to be indignant against those who despise it. How greatly would not a prince think himself offended, if he should call one of his vassals to serve him near his person, and this vassal should refuse to obey the call! And should God not resent such conduct? Oh, he resents it but too much, and threatens such persons by saying, Woe to him that gainsayeth his maker. The word Woe in Scripture signifies eternal damnation. The chastisement of the disobedient will begin even in this life, in which he will always be unquiet, for, says Job, Who hath resisted Him and hath had peace? Therefore he will be deprived of those abundant and efficacious helps necessary to lead a good life. For which reason Habert, a divine, writes, "He will with great difficulty be able to work out his salvation." He will with great difficulty save himself; for, being like a member out of his proper place, he will with great difficulty be able to live well. "In the body of the Church," adds the learned author, "He will be like a limb of the human body out of its place, which may be able to perform its functions, but only with difficulty and in an awkward manner." Whence he concludes, "And though, absolutely speaking, he may be saved, he will with difficulty enter upon and advance in the road, and use the means of salvation." The same thing is taught by St. Bernard and St. Leo. St.- Gregory, writing to the Emperor Maurice, who by an edict had forbidden soldiers to become religious, says that this was an unjust law, which shut the gates of paradise to many, because many would save themselves in religion who would otherwise perish in the world.

Remarkable is the case related by F. Lancicius. There was in the Roman college a youth of great talents. Whilst he was making the spiritual exercises, he asked his confessor whether it was a sin not to correspond with the vocation to the religious life. The confessor replied that in itself it was no grievous sin, because this is a thing of counsel and not of precept, but that one would expose one's salvation to great danger, as it had happened to many, who for this reason were finally damned. He did not obey the call. He went to study in Macerata, where he soon began to omit prayer and holy Communion, and finally gave himself up to a bad life. Soon after, coming one night from the house of a wicked woman, he was mortally wounded by a rival; certain priests ran to his assistance, but he expired before they arrived, and, moreover, in front of the college. By this circumstance God wished to show that this chastisement came upon him for having neglected his vocation.

Remarkable also is the vision had by a novice, who, as F. Pinamonti relates in his treatise of the victorious vocation, had resolved on leaving his Order. He saw Christ on a throne in wrath, ordering his name to be blotted out of the book of life; by this vision he was so terrified that he persevered in his vocation.

How many other similar examples are there, not to be found in books! And how many unhappy youths shall we not see damned on the day of judgment for not having followed their vocation! Such are rebels to the divine light, as the Holy Ghost says: They have been rebellious to the light, they have not known his ways, and they will be justly punished by losing the light; and because they would not walk in the way shown them by the Lord, they shall walk without light in that chosen by their own caprice and perish. Behold, I will utter my spirit to you. Behold the vocation, but because they fail to follow it, God adds: Because I called and you refused . . . you have despised all my counsel . . . I also will laugh in your destruction, and I will mock when that shall come upon you which you feared. Then shall they call upon me, and I will not hear: they shall rise in morning and shall not find me. Because they have hated instruction and received not the fear of the Lord. Nor consented to my counsel, but despised all my reproof. And this signifies that God will not hear the prayers of him who has neglected to obey his voice. St. Augustine says, "They who have despised the will of God which invited them, shall feel the will of God when it becomes its own avenger.

2. WE MUST OBEY THE VOICE OF GOD WITHOUT DELAY.

Whenever God calls to a more perfect state, he who does not wish to expose his eternal salvation to great danger must then obey, and obey promptly. Otherwise he will hear from Jesus Christ the reproach be made to that young man who, when invited to follow him, said, I will follow Thee, Lord, but let me first take my leave of them that are at my house. And Jesus replied to him that he was not fit for paradise: No man putting his hand to the plough and looking back is fit for the kingdom of God.

The lights which God gives are transient, not permanent, gifts. Whence St. Thomas says that the vocation of God to a more perfect life ought to be followed as promptly as possible. He proposes in his summary the question whether it be praiseworthy to enter religion without having asked the counsel of many and without long deliberation? He answers in the affirmative, saying that counsel and deliberation are necessary in doubtful things, but not in this matter Which is certainly good; because Jesus Christ has counselled it in the Gospel, since the religious state comprehends most of the counsels of Jesus Christ. How singular a thing it is, when there is question of entering religion to lead a life more perfect and more free from the dangers of the world, the men of the world say that it is necessary to deliberate a long time before putting such resolutions in execution, in order to ascertain whether the vocation comes from God or from the devil. But they do not talk thus when one is to accept of a place in the magistracy, of a bishopric, etc., where there are so many dangers of losing the soul. Then they do not say that many proofs are required whether there be a true vocation from God.

The saints, however, do not talk thus. St. Thomas says that if the vocation to religion should even come from the devil, we should nevertheless follow it, as a good counsel, though coming from an enemy. St. John Chrysostom, as quoted by the same St. Thomas, says that God, when he gives such vocations, wills that we should not defer even a moment to follow them. Christ requires from us such an obedience that we should not delay an instant. And why this? Because as much as God is pleased to see in a soul promptitude in obeying him, so much he opens his hand and fills it with his blessings. On the contrary, tardiness in obeying him displeases him, and then he shuts his hand and withdraws his lights, so that in consequence a soul will follow its vocation with difficulty and abandon it again easily. Therefore, St. John Chrysostom says that when the devil cannot bring one to give up his resolution of consecrating himself to God, he at least seeks to make him defer the execution of it, and esteems it a great gain if he can obtain the delay of one day only, or even of an hour. Because, after that day or that hour, other occasions presenting themselves, it will be less difficult for him to obtain greater delay, until the individual who has been thus called, finding himself more feeble and less assisted by grace, gives way altogether and loses his vocation. Therefore St. Jerome gives to those who are called to quit the world this advice: "Make haste, I beseech you, and rather cut than loosen the cable by which your bark is bound fast to the land." The saint wishes to say that as a man who should find himself in a boat on the point of sinking, would seek to cut the rope, rather than to loosen it, so he who finds himself in the midst of the world ought to seek to get out of it as promptly as possible, in order to free himself from the danger, which is so great in the world, of losing his own soul.

Let us also hear what St. Francis de Sales writes in his works, on religious vocation, because the whole of it will go to confirm what has already been said, and what will be said hereafter: "To have a sign of a true vocation, it is not necessary that our constancy be sensible, it suffices if it be in the superior part of our soul. And therefore we must not judge that a vocation is not a true one, if the individual thus called, before putting it in execution, does not feel any longer those sensible movements which he felt in the beginning. Even should he feel a repugnance and coldness, which sometimes bring him to waver, and make it appear to him that all is lost. It is enough that the will remains constant in not abandoning the divine call, and also that there remains some affection for this call. To know whether God will have one become a religious, one ought not to expect that God himself should speak or send to one an angel from heaven to signify his will. And as little necessary is it that ten or twelve Doctors should examine whether the vocation is to be followed or not. But it is necessary to correspond with the first movement of the inspiration, and to cultivate it, and then not to grow weary if disgust or coldness should come on; for if one acts thus, God will not fail to make all succeed to his glory. Nor ought we to care much from what quarter the first movement comes. The Lord has many means to call his servants. Sometimes he makes use of a sermon, at other times of the reading of good books. Some, as St. Anthony and St. Francis, have been called by hearing the words of the Gospel; others by means of afflictions and troubles that came upon them in the world, and which suggested to them the motive for leaving it. These persons, although they come to God only because they are disgusted with the world or out of favor with it, nevertheless, failing not to give themselves to him with their whole will, become sometimes greater saints than those who entered religion with a more apparent vocation. Father Flatus relates that a nobleman, riding one day on a fine horse, and striving to make a great display in order to please some ladies whom he saw, was thrown from the horse into the mire, from which he rose besmeared and covered with mud. He was so full of confusion at this accident that at the same moment he resolved to become a religious, saying, 'Treacherous world, thou hast mocked me, but I will mock thee. Thou hast played me a game, I will play thee another; for I will have no more peace with thee, and from this hour I resolve to forsake thee and to become a friar.' And, in fact, he became a religious, and lived in religion a holy life.

III.

Means to be Employed for Preserving a Religious Vocation in the World.

He, then, who wishes to be faithful to the divine call ought not only to resolve to follow it, but to follow it promptly, if he does not wish to expose himself to the evident danger of losing his vocation; and in case he should by necessity be forced to wait, he ought to use all diligence to preserve it, as the most precious jewel he could have.

The means to preserve vocation are three in number: secrecy, prayer, and recollection.

I. SECRECY.

First, generally speaking, he must keep his vocation secret from everybody except his spiritual Father, because commonly the men of the world scruple not to say to young men, who are called to the religious state, that one may serve God everywhere, and therefore in the world also. And it is wonderful that such propositions come sometimes out of the mouth of priests, and even of religious; but of such religious only as have either become so without vocation, or do not know what vocation is. Yes, without doubt, he who is not called to the religious state may serve God in every place, but not he who is called to it, and then from his own inclination wishes to remain in the world; such a one, as I have said above, can with difficulty serve God and lead a good life.

It is especially necessary to keep the vocation secret from parents.

It was, indeed, the opinion of Luther, as Bellarmine relates, that children entering religion without the consent of their parents commit a sin. For, said he children are bound to obey their parents in all things. But this opinion has generally been rejected by Councils and the holy Fathers. The tenth Council of Toledo expressly says: " It is lawful for children to become religious without the consent of their parents, provided they have attained the age of puberty;" these are the words: "It shall not be lawful for parents to put their children in a religious order after they have attained their fourteenth year. After this age, it shall be lawful for children to take upon themselves the yoke of religious observance, whether it be with the consent of their parents, or only the wish of their own hearts." The same is prescribed in the Council of Tribur, and is taught by St. Ambrose, St. Jerome, St. Augustine, St. Bernard, St. Thomas, and others, with St. John Chrysostom, who writes in general: "When parents stand in the way in spiritual things, they ought not even to be recognized."

Some Doctors then say that when a child called by God to the religious state could easily and securely obtain the consent of his parents, without any danger on their part of hindering him from following his vocation, it is becoming that he should seek to obtain their blessing. This doctrine could be held speculatively, but not so in practice, because in practice such a danger always exists. It will be well to discuss this point fully, in order to do away with certain pharisaical scruples which some entertain.

It is certain that in the choice of a state of life, children are not bound to obey parents. Thus the Doctors, with common accord, teach with St. Thomas, who says: "Servants are not bound to obey their masters, nor children their parents, with regard to contracting matrimony, preserving virginity, and such like things. Nevertheless, with regard to the state of marriage, F. Pinamonti, in his treatise on religious vocation, is justly of the opinion of Sanchez, Comminchio, and others, who hold that a child is bound to take counsel of his parents, because in such it matters they may have more experience than the young. But speaking then of religious vocation, the above-mentioned Pinamonti wisely adds that a child is not bound at all to take counsel of his parents, because in this matter they have not any experience, and through interest are commonly changed into enemies, as St. Thomas also remarks, when speaking of religious vocation. "Frequently," he says, "Our friends according to the flesh are opposed to our spiritual good." For fathers often prefer that their children should be damned with themselves, rather than be saved away from them. Whence St. Bernard exclaims, "O hard father, O cruel mother, whose consolation is the death of their son, who wish rather that we perish with them than reign without them!"

God, says a grave author, Porrecta, when he calls one to a perfect life, wishes one to forget one's father, saying, Hearken, O daughter, and see, and incline thine ear; and forget thy people and thy fathers house. "By this, then," he adds, "The Lord certainly admonishes us that he who is called ought by no means to allow the counsel of parents to intervene.""If God will have a soul, who is called by him, forget its father and its father's house, without doubt he suggests by this, that he who is called to the religious state ought not, before he follows the call, to interpose the counsel of the carnal friends of his household."

St. Cyril, explaining what Jesus Christ said to the youth mentioned above, No man putting his hand to the plough and looking back is fit for the kingdom of God, comments on it and says that he who asks for time to confer with his parents in reference to his vocation is exactly the one who is declared by our Lord to be unfit for heaven. "In order to confer with his parents, he looks back who seeks for delay." Whence St. Thomas absolutely advises those who are called to religion, to abstain from deliberating on their vocation with their relatives: "From this deliberation, the relatives of the flesh are before all to be excluded; for it is said, Treat thy cause with thy friend (Prov. 25:9); but the relatives of the flesh are in this affair not our friends, but our enemies, according to the saying of our Lord: A man's enemies are those of his household. (Matt. 10:36).

16

If, then, for following one's vocation it would be a great error to ask the counsel of parents, it would be a greater one still to ask their permission, and to wait for it, for such a demand cannot be made without an evident danger of losing the vocation, as often as there is a probable fear that parents would exert themselves to prevent it. And, in fact, the saints, when they were called to leave the world, left their homes without giving their parents so much as an intimation of it. Thus acted St. Thomas Aquinas, St. Francis Xavier, St. Philip Neri, St. Louis Bertrand. And we know that the Lord has even by miracles approved of these glorious flights.

St. Peter of Alcantara, when he went to the monastery to become a religious, and was fleeing from the house of his mother, under whose obedience he had lived since the death of his father, found himself prevented by a wide river from advancing any farther. He recommended himself to God, and at the same instant saw himself transported to the other side.

Likewise, when St. Stanislaus Kostka fled from home, without the permission of his father, his brother set out after him in great haste in a carriage, but having almost overtaken him, the horses, in spite of all the violence used against them, would not advance a step farther, till turning towards the city, they began to run at full speed.

In like manner the Blessed Oringa of Waldrano, in Tuscany, being promised in marriage to a young man, fled from the house of her parents in order to consecrate herself to God; but the river Arno opposing itself to her course, after a short prayer she saw it divide and form, as it were, two walls of crystal, to let her pass through with dry feet.

Therefore, my very beloved brother, if you are called by God to leave the world, be very careful not to make your resolution known to your parents, and, content to be thus blessed by God, seek to execute it as promptly as you can, and without their knowledge, if you would not expose yourself to the great danger of losing your vocation. For, generally speaking, relatives, as has been said above, especially fathers and mothers, oppose the execution of such resolutions; and although they may be endowed with piety, interest and passion nevertheless render them so blind that under various pretexts they scruple not to thwart with all their might the vocation of their children.

We read in the life of Father Paul Segneri the younger that his mother, though a matron much given to prayer, left nevertheless no means untried to prevent her son from entering the religious state to which he was called. We also read in the life of Mgr. Cavalieri, Bishop of Troja, that his father, although a man of great piety, used every means to prevent his son from entering the Congregation of Pious Workmen (which, notwithstanding, he afterwards did), and even went so far as to bring against him a lawsuit in the ecclesiastical court. And how many other fathers, notwithstanding they were men of piety and prayer, have not in such cases been seen to change, and to become possessed, as it were, of the devil! For under no other circumstance does hell seem to employ more formidable arms than when there is question of preventing those who are called to the religious state from executing their resolution.

For this reason be also very careful not to communicate your design to your friends, who will not scruple to dissuade you from it, or at least to divulge the secret, so that the knowledge of it will easily come to the ears of your parents.

18

2. PRAYER.

In the second place, it is necessary to know that these vocations are only preserved by prayer; he who gives up prayer will certainly give up his vocation. It is necessary to pray, and to pray much; and therefore let him who feels himself called, not omit to make every morning after rising an hour of mental prayer, or at least half an hour, in his own room, if he can do so there without molestation, and if not, in the church, and likewise half an hour in the evening.

Let him not neglect also to make every day, without fail, a visit to the Most Holy Sacrament, as also to the Most Blessed Virgin Mary, in order to obtain the grace of perseverance in his vocation. Let him likewise not omit to receive Holy Communion thrice, or at least twice, a week.

His meditations ought almost always to be on this point of the vocation, considering how great a favor from God he has- received in being thus called by him; how much more easily he will secure his eternal salvation, if he be faithful to God in following his vocation; and, on the contrary, to how great a danger of being damned he exposes himself if he be unfaithful. Let him then especially place before his eyes the hour of death, and consider the contentment that he will then feel if he shall have obeyed God, and the pains and the remorse he would experience if he should die in the world. To this end I shall add at the end of this some considerations on which he may make his mental prayer.

It is, moreover, necessary that all his prayers to Jesus and Mary, and especially those after Communion and in the visits, be directed to obtain perseverance. In all his prayers and Communions let him always renew the offering of himself to God, by saying, "Behold, O Lord! I am no more mine, I am Thine. Already have I given myself to Thee, and now I renew this my offering of my whole self. Accept of me and give me strength to be faithful to Thee and to retire as quickly as possible into Thy house."

3. RECOLLECTION.

In the third place, it is necessary that he be recollected, which will not be possible for him unless he withdraws from worldly conversations and amusements. What, in short, as long as we are in the world, is enough to cause the loss of vocation? A mere nothing. One day of amusement, a word from a friend, a passion we do not mortify, a little attachment, a thought of fear, a resentment we do not overcome, suffices to bring to nought all our resolutions of retiring from the world, or of giving ourselves entirely to God. Wherefore we ought to keep perfectly recollected, detaching ourselves from everything of this world. We ought during this time to think of nothing but prayer and frequenting the sacraments, and to be nowhere but at home and in church. Let him who will not do so, but distracts himself by pastimes, be persuaded that he will without doubt lose his vocation. He will remain with the remorse of not having followed it, but he certainly will not follow it. Oh, how many by neglecting these precautions have lost, first their vocation, and afterwards their souls!

IV.

Disposition required for entering Religion.

He who feels himself to be called by God to a religious Institute in which reigns exact observance ought to know that the end of every regular observance is, to follow as exactly as possible the footsteps and examples of the most holy life of Jesus Christ, who led a life entirely detached and mortified, full of suffering and contempt. He, then, who resolves to enter such a holy state must at the same time resolve to enter it for the sake of suffering and denying himself in all things, as Jesus Christ himself has declared to those who wish perfectly to follow him– If any man will come after Me, let him deny himself, and take up his cross and follow Me. He, then, who wishes to enter religion must firmly establish within himself this resolution to go to suffer, and to suffer much, so that afterwards he may not give way to temptations, when, having entered, he feels depressed under the hardships and privations of the poor and mortified life which is there led.

Many, on entering Communities of exact observance take not the proper means of finding peace therein, and of becoming saints, because they only place before their eyes the advantages of the Community life, such as the solitude, the quiet, the freedom from the troubles caused by relatives, from strife and other disagreeable matters, and from the cares consequent on being obliged to think of one's lodging, food, and clothing.

There is no doubt that every religious is only too much indebted to his Order, which delivers him from so many troubles, and thus procures for him so great a facility to serve God perfectly in peace, continually furnishing him with so many means for the welfare of his soul, so many good examples from his companions, so much good advice from his Superiors who watch for his benefit, so many exercises conducive to eternal salvation. All this is true; but with all this he must also, in order not to be deprived of so blessed a lot, resolve to embrace all the sufferings he may,

21

on the other hand, meet with in the Order; for if he does not embrace them with love, he will never obtain that full peace which God gives to those who overcome themselves: To him that overcomes I will give the hidden manna. For the peace which God gives his faithful servants to taste is hidden; nor is it known by the men of the world, who, seeing their mortified life, know not how to envy them, but pity them and call them the unhappy ones of this earth. But "They see the cross, the unction they do not see," a says St. Bernard; they see their mortification, but they do not see the contentment that God gives them to enjoy.

It is true that in the spiritual life one has to suffer, but says St. Teresa, when one resolves to suffer, the pain is gone. Nay, the pains themselves turn into joy. "My daughter," so the Lord said one day to St. Bridget, " the treasure of my graces seems to be surrounded with thorns; but for him who overcomes the first stings, all is changed into sweetness." And then those delights which God gives to his beloved souls to enjoy in their prayers, in their Communions, in their solitude; those lights, those holy ardors and embraces, that quiet of conscience, that blessed hope of eternal life, who can ever understand them, if he does not experience them? "One drop of the consolations of God," said St. Teresa, "Is worth more than all the consolations and the pleasures of the world." Our most gracious God knows well how to give to him who suffers something for his sake, even in this valley of tears, the experience of the fore taste of the glory of the blessed; for in this is properly verified that which David says: Thou who framest labor in commandment. In the spiritual life, God, announcing pains, tediousness, death, seems to frame labor, but, in fact, afterwards it is not so; for spiritual life brings to them who entirely give themselves to God that peace which, as St. Paul says, Surpasseth all understanding. It surpasses all the pleasures of the world and of world-lings. Whence we see a religious more content in a poor cell than all the monarchs in their royal palaces. O taste, and see that the Lord is sweet.

But, on the other hand, he must be persuaded that he who does not resolve to suffer and to overcome himself in the things contrary to his inclinations, will never be able to enjoy this true peace, though he should have already entered religion. To him that overcomes, I will give the hidden manna. It is, then, necessary that he who wishes to be admitted into an Order of exact observance should enter with a mind determined to overcome himself in everything, by expelling from his heart every inclination and desire that is not from God, nor for God, so that he must detach himself from all things, and especially from the four following: 1.. From his comforts. 2. From his parents. 3. From self–esteem. 4. From his own will.

1. DETACHMENT FROM HIS COMFORTS.

In religion, after the year of novitiate, one makes, besides the vows of chastity and obedience, also the vow of poverty, in consequence of which one can never possess anything as one's individual property, not even a pin, no income, no money or other things. The Community will provide him with all that he needs. But the vow of poverty does not suffice to make one a true follower of Jesus Christ if one does not afterwards embrace with joy of spirit all the inconveniences of poverty. "Not poverty, but the love of poverty is a virtue," says St. Bernard, and he means to say that for one to become a saint it is not enough to be poor only, if one does not love also the inconveniences of poverty. "Oh, how many would wish to be poor and similar to Jesus Christ!"

23

says Thomas à Kempis; "They wish to be poor but without any want," but so that they be in want of nothing. In a word, they would wish the honor and the reward of poverty, but not the inconveniences of poverty.

It is easy to understand that in religion no one will seek for things that are superfluous,— cloths of silk, costly food, furniture of value, and the like; but he may desire to have all things that are necessary, and these he may be unable to get. For then it is he gives proof that he truly loves poverty, when things that are needful,— such as his necessary clothing, bed-covering or food, happen to be wanting, and yet he remains content and is not troubled. And what kind of poverty would that be to suffer if he were never in want of anything necessary? F. Balthasar Alvarez says that in order truly to love poverty we must also love the effects of poverty; that is, as he enumerates them, cold, hunger, thirst, and contempt.

In religion, every one ought not only to be content with that which is given to him, without ever asking for anything of which, through the neglect of the stewards, he should be in want, which would be a great defect, but he ought also to prepare himself sometimes to bear the want even of those simple things that the Rule allows. For it may happen that sometimes he is in want of clothes, coverings, linen, or such—like things, and then he has to be satisfied with that lit-tle which has been given him, without complaining or being disquieted at seeing himself in want even of what is neces-sary. He who has not this spirit, let him not think of entering religion, because this is a sign that he is not called thereto or that he has not the will to embrace the spirit of the Insti-tute. He who goes to serve God in his house, says St. Teresa, ought to consider that he is going not to be well treated for God, but to suffer for God.

2. DETACHMENT FROM HIS PARENTS.

He who wishes to enter religion must detach himself from his parents and forget them altogether. For, in religious houses of exact observance, detachment from parents is put in practice in the highest degree, in order perfectly to follow the doctrine of Jesus Christ, who said, I came not to send peace, but the sword: I came to set a man at variance with his father, etc.; and then added the reason: A man's enemies shall be they of his own household. And this is especially the case, as has been remarked above, in this point of religious vocation. When one's leaving the world is in question, there are no worse enemies than parents, who, either through interest of passion, prefer to become enemies of God, by turning their children away from their vocation, rather than to give their consent to it. Oh, how many parents shall we see in the valley of Josaphat damned for having made their children or nephews lose their vocation! And how many youths shall we see damned who, in order to please their parents, and by not detaching themselves from them, have lost their vocation and afterwards their souls! Whence Jesus declares to us, If any man hate not his father, etc., he cannot be my disciple. Let him, then, who wishes to enter a religious Order of perfect observance, and to become a true disciple of Jesus Christ, resolve to forget his parents altogether.

When any one has already entered religion, let him remember that he must practise then the same detachment from parents. Let him know that he cannot go to visit his parents in their own house, except in the case of some dangerous illness of his father or mother, or of some other urgent necessity, though always with the permission of the Superior, Otherwise to go to the house of one's parents without the most express permission would be considered in religion as a most notable and scandalous fault. In religion it is also considered a great defect even to ask permission or to show a desire of seeing parents or of speaking with them.

St. Charles Borromeo said that when he visited the house of his parents he always, after his return, found himself less fervent in spirit. And thus, let him who goes to the house of his parents by his own will and not through a positive obedience to his Superiors, be persuaded that he will leave it either under temptation or be cold and lukewarm.

St. Vincent of Paul could only be induced once to visit his country and his parents, and this out of pure necessity; and he said that the love of home and country was a great impediment to his spiritual progress. He said also that many, on account of having visited their country, had become so tender towards their relatives that they were like flies, which being once entangled in a cobweb, cannot extricate themselves from it. He added, "For that one time that I went, though it was for a short time only, and though I took care to prevent in my relatives every hope of help from me, notwithstanding, I felt at leaving them such a pain that I ceased not to weep all along the road, and was for three months harassed by the thought of succoring them. Finally, God in his mercy took that temptation from me."

Let him know, moreover, that no one may write to his parents without permission, and without showing the letter to the Superior. Otherwise, he would be guilty of a most grievous fault that is not to be tolerated in religion, and should be punished with severity; for from this might come a thousand disorders tending to destroy the religious spirit. Let especially the new–comer know that during the novitiate this is observed with the greatest rigor; for novices during their year of novitiate do not easily obtain permission to talk to their parents, or to write to them.

Finally, let him know that in case a subject should become sick, it would be a notable defect to ask or to show an inclination to go to his own house for his restoration to health, under the plea of being better taken care of, or of enjoying the benefit of his native air. The air of his own country becomes almost always, or rather always, hurtful, and pestilential to the spirit of the subject. And if he should ever say that he wishes to be cured at home in order not to subject the Order to expenses for remedies, let him know that the Order has charity enough to take sufficient care of the sick. As to the change of air, the Superiors will think of that; and if that of one house is not beneficial to him, they will send him to another. And as for remedies, they will even sell the books, if need be, to provide for the sick. And so let him be sure that divine Providence will not fail him. And if the Lord should decree against his recovery, he ought to conform to the will of God, without even mentioning the word "Home." The greatest grace that he who enters an Order can desire is to die, when God wills it, in the house of God, assisted by the brethren of his Order, and not in a secular house in the midst of his relatives.

3. DETACHMENT FROM SELF-ESTEEM.

He must also be altogether detached from all self–esteem. Many leave their country, their comforts, and parents, but carry with them a certain esteem for themselves; but this is the most hurtful attachment of all. The greatest sacrifice that we can make to God is to give to him not only goods, pleasures, and home, but ourselves also, by leaving ourselves. This is that denying of one's self which Jesus Christ

27

recommends above all to his followers. And in order to deny one's self, one must first place under foot all self–esteem, by desiring and embracing every imaginable contempt that he may meet with in religion; as, for instance, to see others, whom perhaps he thinks less deserving, preferred to himself, or to be considered unfit to be employed, or only employed in lower and more laborious occupations. He ought to know that in the house of God those charges are the highest and the most honorable that are imposed by obedience. God forbid that any one should seek for or aspire to any office or charge of pre-eminence. This would be a strange thing in religion, and he would be noted as proud and ambitious, and as such should be put in penance, and should especially be mortified in this point. Better would it be, perhaps, that a religious Order should be destroyed than that there should enter into it that accursed pest of ambition which, when it enters, disfigures the most exemplary Communities, and the most beautiful works of God.

But he ought to feel even consoled in spirit when he sees himself mocked and despised by his companions. I say consoled in spirit, for as to the flesh this will be impossible, nor need a subject be uneasy when he sees that he resents it; it is enough that the spirit embraces it, and that he rejoices at it in the superior part of the soul. Thus also seeing himself continually reprimanded and mortified by all, not only by Superiors, but also by equals and inferiors, he ought heartily, and with a tranquil mind, to thank those who thus reprimand him, and have the charity to admonish him, answering that he will be more attentive not to fall into that fault again.

One of the greatest desires of the saints in this world was to be contemned for the love of Jesus Christ. It was this that St. John of the Cross asked for, when Jesus Christ appeared to him with a cross on his shoulder, and said, "John, ask from me what thou wishest," and St. John answered, "O Lord, to suffer and to be despised for Thee." The Doctors teach, with St. Francis de Sales, that the highest degree of humility we can have is to be pleased with abjections and humiliations. And in this consists also one of the greatest merits we can have with God. One contempt suffered in peace for the love of God is of greater value in his sight than a thousand disciplines and a thousand fasts.

It is necessary to know that to suffer contempt either from Superiors or from companions is a thing unavoidable even in the most holy Communities. Read the lives of the saints, and you will see how many mortifications were encountered by St. Francis Regis, St. Francis of Jerome, Father Torres, and others. The Lord sometimes permits that even among saints there should exist, though without their fault, certain natural antipathies, or at least a certain diversity of character among subjects of the greatest piety, which will cause them to suffer many contradictions. At other times false reports will be spread and believed. God himself will permit this, in order that the subjects may have occasion to exercise themselves in patience and humility.

In short, he will gain little in religion and lose much who cannot quietly put up with contempt and contradiction; and, therefore, he who enters religion to give himself entirely to God ought to be ashamed not to know how to bear contempt when he appears before Jesus Christ, who was "Filled with opprobriums" for love of us. Let everyone be attentive to this, and resolve to be pleased in religion with all abjections, and to prepare himself to suffer many of them, for without the least doubt he will have many to bear. Otherwise, the disquiet caused by contradictions, and contempt badly borne with, might trouble him so much as to make him lose his vocation, and chase him out of religion. Oh, how many have lost their vocation on account of such impatience in humiliations! But of what service to the Order or to God can he be who does not know how to bear contempt for his sake? And how can one ever be said to be dead according to that promise which he made to Jesus Christ, on entering religion, to die to himself if he remained alive to resentment and disquiet, when he sees himself humbled? Out of the Order with such subjects, so attached to their own esteem, out with them! It is well for them to go as soon as possible, that they may not infect the rest also with their pride. In religion every one ought to be dead, and especially to his own self–esteem, otherwise it is better for him not to enter, or to depart again if he has already entered.

4. DETACHMENT FROM HIS OWN WILL.

He who enters religion must altogether renounce his own will, consecrating it entirely to holy obedience. Of all things, this is the most necessary. What does it avail to leave comforts, parents, and honors, if we still carry into religion our own will? In this principally consists the denial of ourselves, the spiritual death, and the entire surrender of ourselves to Jesus Christ. The gift of the heart–that is, of the will–is what pleases him most, and what he wishes from the children of religion. Otherwise, if we do not entirely detach ourselves from our own will and renounce it in all, all mortifications, all meditations and prayers, and all other sacrifices, will be of little avail.

It is, then, evident that this is the greatest merit we can have before God, and this is the only and sure way of pleasing

God in all things, so that then we can, each one of us, say what Jesus our Saviour said: I do always the things that please Him. Certainly, he who in religion lives without self–will may say and hope that in all that he does he pleases God, whether he studies or prays, or hears confessions, whether he goes to the refectory or to recreation, or to rest; for in religion not a step is made, not a breath drawn, but in obedience to the Rule, or to Superiors.

The world does not know, and even certain persons given to spirituality have little idea of, the great value of a Community life under obedience. It is true that outside of religious Communities there are to be found many persons who do much, and, may be, more than those who live under obedience; they preach, do penance, pray and fast, but in all this they consult more or less their own will. God grant that at the day of judgment they may not have to lament as those mentioned in Scripture: Why have we fasted and Thou hast not regarded, have we humbled ourselves, and Thou hast not taken notice? Behold, in the day of your fast, your own will is found. On which passage St. Bernard remarks: "Self–will is a great evil, for through it that which is good in itself may be for you no good at all." This to be understood when in all these exercises we seek not God, but ourselves. On the contrary, he who does all by obedience is sure that in all he pleases God. The Venerable Mother Mary of Jesus said that she prized so much her vocation to religion principally for two reasons: the first was that in the monastery she enjoyed always the presence and company of Jesus in the Blessed Sacrament, and the other was that there by obedience she entirely belonged to God, sacrificing to him her own will.

It is related by F. Rodriguez that after the death of Dositheus, the disciple of St. Dorotheas, the Lord revealed that in those five years he had lived under obedience, though by reason of his infirmities he could not practise the austerities of the other monks, yet by the virtue of obedience he had merited the reward of St. Paul the Hermit and of St. Anthony the Abbot.

He, then, who wishes to enter religion must resolve to renounce altogether his own will, and to will only what holy obedience wills. God preserve any religious from ever letting escape from his mouth the words, I will or I will not. But in all things, even when asked by Superiors what he desires, he should only answer, I wish that which holy obedience wills. And, provided there is no evident sin, he ought in every command imposed on him to obey blindly and without examination, because the duty of examining and deciding the doubts belongs not to him, but to his Superiors. Otherwise, if in obeying he does not submit his own judgment to that of the Superior, his obedience is imperfect. St. Ignatius of Loyola said that prudence in things of obedience is not required in subjects, but in Superiors; and if there is prudence in obeying, it is to obey without prudence. St. Bernard says, "Perfect obedience is indiscreet," and in another place he says, "For a prudent novice to remain in the Congregation is an impossible thing;" and, adding the reason for it, he says, "To judge belongs to the Superior; and to obey, to the subject."

But to make progress in this virtue of obedience, on which all depends, he must always keep his mind ready to do all that for which he feels the greatest repugnance, and, on the contrary, he must be prepared to bear it quietly when he sees that all he seeks or desires is refused to him. It will happen that when he wishes to be in solitude, to apply himself to prayer or study, he will be the most employed in exterior occupations. For though it is true that in religion one leads as much as possible a solitary life when at home, and that for this end there are many hours of silence, the retreat each year of ten days in perfect silence,– and of one day each month, besides the fifteen days before the receiving of the habit, and one of fifteen before the profession, when the vows are made,–nevertheless, if it is an Order of priests called to work and to be employed for the salvation of souls, the subject, if he is continually employed in this by obedience, ought to be content with the prayers and exercises of the Community; he must be prepared sometimes to go even without these when obedience will have it so, without either excusing himself or being disquieted, being well persuaded of that of which St. Mary Magdalene of Pazzi was so confident when she said that "All the things which are done through obedience are but so many prayers."

V.

Trials which we must expect
to have in the Religious Life.

When, then, any one has thus entered religion, however truly he may be called, and though he may have conquered all his passions and his earthly affections, let him not imagine that he will be exempt from other temptations and trials, which God himself will send him, such as tediousness, darkness, various fears, in order to establish him more firmly in his vocation. We must remember that even the saints, who have loved their vocation the most, have sometimes suffered great darkness with regard to it, and that it seemed to them as if they were deceived, and would not be able to save themselves in that state. So it happened with St. Teresa, St. John of the Cross, the Venerable Mother Frances de Chantal. But by recommending themselves to God, that darkness was dissipated, and they recovered their peace of mind. Thus the Lord tries his most beloved children, as it was said to Tobias: Because thou wast acceptable to God, it was necessary that temptation should prove thee. And in the book of Deuteronomy, The Lord, your God trieth you, that it may appear whether you love him or not. Let each one therefore prepare himself to suffer in religion this obscurity. It will sometimes appear to him that he cannot bear the observance of the Order, that he will have no more peace of mind, or will not even be able to save himself. But, most of all, everyone must be on his guard when the temptation presents specious scruples or pretexts of greater spiritual good, in order to make him abandon his vocation.

The principal remedies in such temptations are two in number.

FIRST REMEDY: TO HAVE RECOURSE TO GOD.

The first is prayer, Go ye to him and be enlightened. For as it will not be possible for temptation to overcome him who has recourse to prayer, so he who does not recommend himself to God will surely be overcome by it. And let it be remarked that sometimes it will not suffice to have recourse to God once, or for a few days, to become victorious. Perhaps the Lord will permit the temptation to continue, even after we have prayed for several weeks, months, and even years; but let us be assured that he who ceases not to recommend himself to God will certainly be enlightened and victorious, and thereafter he will have more peace and be more firm in his vocation.

Until we have gone through that storm, which for the most part comes over all, let none of us think himself secure. Let

34

us be persuaded, however, that in this time of temptation we ought not to expect a fervor, and a clearness of reason sufficient to tranquillize ourselves; for in the midst of this darkness we see nothing but confusion. We have nothing then to do but to say to the Lord, O Lord, help me! O Lord, help me and also to have frequently recourse to Most Holy Mary, who is the mother of perseverance, confiding in that divine promise: Ask and you shall receive. And it is certain that he who, with the help of divine grace, is victorious in such a combat finds afterwards a double calm and peace in his vocation.

SECOND REMEDY:
TO HAVE RECOURSE TO THE SUPERIORS.

The second remedy, and a principal and necessary one in such temptations, is to communicate to the Superiors, or to the spiritual Father of the Community, the temptation which afflicts you, and this at once, before the temptation becomes strong. St. Philip Neri said that when a temptation is thus manifested it is half vanquished. On the contrary, there is in such a case no greater evil than to conceal the temptation from Superiors; for then, on the one hand, God withdraws his light because of the little fidelity shown by the subject in not disclosing it, and, on the other, whilst the mine is not sprung, the temptation gains strength. Whence it may be held for certain that he will surely lose his vocation who, when he is tempted against it, does not disclose his temptations.

And let it be understood that in religion the most dangerous temptations that hell can bring against a subject are those against vocation, in which, if it should succeed and conquer, by that one stroke it will have gained many victories; for when a subject has lost his vocation and left religion, what good will he any more be able to do in the service of God? Though the enemy may make him believe that out of religion he will have more peace and be able to do more good, nevertheless let him hold for certain that as soon as he is out of it he will feel such a remorse in his heart that he will nevermore have peace. And God grant that such a remorse may not torment him afterwards through all eternity in hell, into which, as has already been said, he who through his own fault loses his vocation falls so very easily. He will be so lukewarm and discouraged in doing good that he will not even have the courage to raise his eyes to heaven. It will be an easy thing for him to give up prayer altogether, because as often as he begins it he will feel a hell of remorse, hearing his con science reproach him, and saying, "What hast thou done? Thou hast abandoned God; thou hast lost thy vocation; and for what? To follow thine own caprice, to please thy parents." Let him be certain that he will have to hear this reproach through his whole life, and still more shall he hear it made to him at the hour of his death, when, in sight of eternity, instead of dying in the house of God, and in–the midst of good brethren in religion, he will have to die outside of the Community, perhaps in his own house, in the midst of his relatives, to please whom he has displeased God. Let religious always beseech God to let them die rather than to permit that greatest of disgraces, the greatness of which they will better understand at the point of death and to their greater torment, because then there will be no more any remedy for their error. For him, then, who is tempted against his vocation, this is the best meditation he can make in the time of the temptation,– namely, to reflect what torment the remorse of having lost his vocation, and of having to die outside of religion, through his own caprice, through his own fault, will cause him at the hour of death.

CONCLUSION.

Finally, let him who wishes to enter religion not forget to resolve to become a saint, and to suffer every exterior and interior pain, in order to be faithful to God, and not to lose his vocation. And if he be not resolved to this, I exhort him not to deceive the Superiors and himself, and not to enter at all, for this is a sign that he is not called, or, which is a still greater evil, that he wishes not to correspond, as he ought, with the grace of his vocation. Hence, with so bad a disposition it is better to remain without, in order to acquire a better disposition, to resolve to give himself entirely to God, and to suffer all for God. Otherwise he will do an injury both to himself and to the Order; for he will easily go back to the world, and then, being disgraced before the world, as well as before God, he will be guilty of a still further infidelity to his vocation, and will lose the confidence in the power of taking another step in the way of God. God only knows into what other misfortunes and sins he may afterwards fall.

On the other hand, a beautiful sight it is to see in religion souls wholly given to God, who live in the world as if out of the world, without any other thought than that of pleasing God.

In religion each one has to live only for eternal life. What happiness for us, if we spend these few days of our life for God! And to this he is most especially obliged who has perhaps already spent much of his life in the service of the world. Let us set eternity before our eyes, and then we shall suffer all with peace and joyfulness.

Let us thank God, who gives us so much light and so many means to serve him perfectly, since he has chosen us, from

37

among so many, to serve him in religion, having bestowed on us the gift of his holy love. Let us make haste to please him in the practice of virtue, reflecting that, as St. Teresa said to her daughters, we have already by his grace done the principal thing necessary to become saints, by turning our backs on the world and all its goods, the least yet, remains to be done, and we shall be saints. I hold it for certain that for those who die in religion, Jesus Christ has prepared a prominent place in paradise. On this earth we shall be poor, despised, and treated as fools, as imprudent men, but in the other life our lot will be changed.

Let us always recommend ourselves to our Redeemer hidden in the Sacrament, and to Most Holy Mary, because in religion all subjects must profess a most special love for Jesus in the Blessed Sacrament, and for the Immaculate Virgin Mary; and let us have great confidence. Jesus Christ has chosen us to be princes of his court, as we may confidently conclude from the protection he extends to all religious Orders, and to each member of them. The Lord is my light and my salvation, whom shall I fear?

O Lord, finish Thy work, and, for Thy glory, grant us to be all Thine, so that all the members of Thy Orders may until the day of judgment, be pleasing to Thee, and gain over to Thee an immense number of souls. Amen. Amen.

CONSIDERATIONS FOR THOSE WHO ARE CALLED TO THE RELIGIOUS STATE.

CONSIDERATION I.

How the Salvation of the Soul is secured by entering the Religious State.

To know how important is the eternal salvation of our soul, it suffices to have faith, and to consider that we have but one soul, and when that is lost, all is lost. What does it profit a man if he gain the whole world, and suffer the loss of his soul? This great maxim of the Gospel has induced many youths either to shut themselves up in cloisters or to live in deserts, or by martyrdom to give up their lives for Jesus Christ. For, said they, what does it profit us to possess the whole world, and all the goods of this world, in this present life, which must soon finish, and then be damned and be miserable in that life to come, which will never end? All those rich men, all those princes and emperors, who are now in hell, what have they now of all they enjoyed in this life, but a greater torment and a greater despair? Miserable beings, they lament now and say, All those things are passed like shadows. For them all is passed like a shadow, like a dream, and that lamentation which is their lot has lasted already many years, and shall last throughout all eternity. The fashion of this world passeth away. This world is a scene which lasts but a short time; happy he who plays on this scene that part which will afterwards make him happy in the life which will never end. When he shall then be contented, honored, and a prince in paradise, so long as God shall be God, little will he care for having been in this world poor, despised, and in tribulation. For this end alone has God placed us on this earth, and keeps us here in life, not to acquire transitory but eternal goods: The end is life everlasting.

This is the sole end, which all men who live in the world ought to have in view. But the misfortune is, that in the world one thinks little or nothing of everlasting life. In the midst of the darkness of this Egypt, the greatest number of men bestow all their care on acquiring honor and pleasures; and this is the reason why so many perish. With desolation is all the land made desolate, because there is none that considereth in his heart. How few are they who reflect on death, by which for us the scene is closed; on the eternity which awaits us; on what God has done for our sake! And thence it comes that these miserable beings live in blindness and at random, far from God, having their eyes, like the beasts, intent only on earthly things, without remembering God, without desiring his love, and without a thought of eternity. Therefore, they die afterwards an unhappy death, which will be the beginning of an eternal death and an endless misery. Having arrived there, they will open their eyes; but it will be only to lament for their own foolishness.

This is the great means of salvation which is found in religion, to wit: the continual meditation on the eternal truths. Remember thy last end, and thou shalt never sin. In all well–regulated religious houses this is done every day, and even several times a day. And therefore in this light of divine things, which there shines continually, it is morally impossible to live, at least for a long time, far from God, and without keeping one's account ready for eternity.

Prayer.

O my God, how have I ever deserved this great mercy, that, having left so many others to live in the midst of the world,

Thou hast willed to call me, who have offended Thee more than others, and deserved, more than they, to be deprived of Thy divine light, to enjoy the honor of living as a friend in Thy own house! O Lord, grant that I may understand this exceeding grace which Thou hast bestowed on me, that I may always thank Thee for it, as I purpose and hope to do always during my life and throughout eternity, and do not permit me to be ungrateful for it. Since Thou hast been so liberal towards me, and hast in Thy love preferred me to others, it is but just that more than others I should serve and love Thee. O my Jesus! Thou wouldst have me to be wholly Thine, and to Thee I give myself wholly. Accept me, and henceforward keep me as Thy own, since I am no more mine. Finish Thou the work which Thou hast begun. Thou hast called me to Thy house, because Thou wilt have me become a saint. Make me then what Thou wilt have me. Do it, O eternal Father, for the love of Jesus Christ, in whom is all my confidence. I love Thee, my sovereign good, I love Thee. O infinite goodness! I love Thee alone, and will love Thee forever. O Mary, my hope, come to my assistance, and obtain for me to be always faithful and thankful to my Lord.

CONSIDERATION II.

The Happy Death of the Religious.

Happy are the dead who die in the Lord. And who are those blessed dead who die in the Lord, but the religious, who at the end of their lives are found already dead to the world, having already detached themselves by their holy vows from the world and all its goods?

Consider, my brother, how content you will feel if, following your vocation, it will be your good fortune to die in the house of God. The devil will certainly represent to you that if you retire into the house of God, you may perhaps afterwards repent of having left your own house and your own country, and deprived your parents of that succor which they might have expected from you. But say to yourself: shall I, at the point of death, repent of having put my resolution in execution, or shall I be content? I beseech you, therefore, to imagine yourself now already at the point of death, about to appear before the tribunal of Jesus Christ. Reflect what then, reduced to that state, you would wish to have done. Perhaps to have contented your parents, to have worked for your own family and your country, and then to die surrounded by brothers, and nephews, and relatives, after having lived in your own house with the title of pastor, of canon, of bishop, of a member of the cabinet, and after having done your own will? Or rather, to die in the house of God, assisted by your good brethren in religion, who encourage you on the great passage to eternity, after having lived many years in religion, humbled, mortified, poor, far from parents, deprived of your own will, and under obedience, and detached from everything in the world,—all these things render death sweet and agreeable? "He who has been accustomed to deprive himself of the delights of the world," says St. Bernard, "Will not regret having done so when he has to leave it." Pope Honorius II., when dying, wished that he had remained in his monastery, occupied in washing the plates, and had not been Pope. Philip II. wished at his death that he had been a lay-brother in some religious order, intent on serving God, and had not been a king. Philip III., also King of Spain, said when he was dying, "Oh that I had been in a desert, there to serve God, and that I had never been a monarch, for had such been the case, I should now appear with more confidence before the tribunal of Jesus Christ."

When, then, hell tempts you about your vocation, think of the hour of death, and set before your eyes that all–important moment "Upon which eternity depends." Thus you will overcome all temptations; you will be faithful to God; and certainly you will not repent of it at the point of death, but will give thanks to the Lord, and die contented. Gerard, brother of St. Bernard, died singing, at the very thought of dying in the house of God.

Father Suarez, of the Company of Jesus, felt at his death so great consolation and sweetness at dying in religion that he said, "I never thought it was so sweet to die."

Another good religious, of the same society, when at the point of death, laughed; and being asked why he laughed, answered: "And why should I not laugh? Has not Jesus Christ himself promised paradise to him who leaves everything for his sake? Was it not he who said, Every one that has left house, or brethren, or father, etc., shall receive a hundred–fold, and shall possess life everlasting? I have left all for God; God is faithful, he cannot fail to fulfil his promises; and so," he said, "Why should I not rejoice and laugh, seeing myself assured of paradise?"

A certain lay–brother, who died some years ago, was asked, at his death, in which house he would rather be. He answered, "I desire nothing but to die and to be united with God."

Father Januarius Sarnelli, a short time before his death, when conversing with God, uttered the following words: "O Lord, Thou knowest that all I have done, all I have thought, has been for Thy glory; now I wish to go to see Thee face to face, if it please Thee so;" then he said, "Come, I will begin a sweet agony;" and began to converse affectionately with

God, and shortly after placidly expired, preserving the smile on his lips, and the body began to give forth a sweet odor, which, as they attested, was perceived for several days in the room in which he had died.

St. Bernard, then, speaking of the happy state of religious, had good reason to exclaim: "O secure life, in which death is expected without fear,—ay, sweetly desired and devoutly accepted!"

Prayer.

O my Lord Jesus Christ, who, in order to obtain a happy death for me, hast chosen so bitter a death for Thyself; since Thou hast loved me to such an extent as to have chosen me to follow more closely Thy holy life, to have me thus more intimately united with Thy loving heart, bind me, I beseech Thee, wholly to Thee with the sweet cords of Thy love, that I may no more separate myself from Thee. O my beloved Redeemer! I wish to be grateful to Thee, and to correspond with Thy grace, but I fear my weakness may render me unfaithful; O my Jesus, do not permit this. Let me die rather than abandon Thee, or forget the peculiar affection Thou hast shown me.

I love Thee, O my dear Saviour! Thou art and shalt always be the only Lord of my heart and of my soul. I leave all and choose Thee alone for my treasure, O most pure Lamb of God, O my most ardent lover! My beloved is white and ruddy, chosen out of thousands. Be gone, ye creatures, my only good is my God, he is my love, my all. I love Thee, O my Jesus, and in loving Thee I will spend the remainder of my life, be it short, or be it long. I embrace Thee, I press Thee to my heart, and I wish to die united with Thee. I wish nothing else. Make me live always burning with Thy love, and when 1 shall have arrived at the end of my life, make me to expire in an ardent act of love towards Thee.

Immaculate Virgin Mary, obtain thou this grace for me, I hope it from thee.

CONSIDERATION III.

The Account which he will have to render to Jesus Christ, on the Day of Judgment, who does not follow his Vocation.

The grace of vocation to the religious state is not an ordinary grace; it is a very rare one, which God grants only to a few. He hath not done so to every nation. Oh, how much greater is this grace, to be called to a perfect life and to become one of the household of God, than if one were called to be the king of any kingdom on this earth, for what comparison can there be between a temporal kingdom of this earth and the eternal kingdom of heaven?

But the greater the grace is, the greater will be the indignation of the Lord against him who has not corresponded with it, and the more rigorous will be his judgment at the day of account. If a king were to call a poor shepherd to his royal palace, to serve him among the noblemen of his court, what would not be the indignation of this king were he to refuse such a favor, through unwillingness to leave his miserable stable and his little flock? God knows well the value of his graces, and therefore he chastises with severity those who despise them. He is the Lord; when he calls, he wishes to be obeyed, and obeyed promptly. When, therefore, by his inspiration, he calls a soul to a perfect life, if it does not correspond, he deprives it of his light, and abandons it to its own darkness. Oh, how many poor souls shall we see among the reprobate on the day of judgment for this very reason, that they were called and would not correspond!

Give thanks, then, to the Lord, who has invited you to follow him; but if you do not correspond, fear. Since God calls you to serve him nearer to his person, it is a sign that he wishes to save you. But he will have you to be saved in that path only which he indicates to you and has chosen for you. If you wish to save yourself on a road of your own choosing, there is great danger that you will not be saved at all; for if you remain in the world, when God wishes you to be a religious, he will not give you those efficacious helps prepared for you had you lived in his house, and without these you will not save yourself. My sheep hear my voice. He who will not obey the voice of God shows that he is not, and will not be, one of his sheep, but in the valley of Josaphat he will be condemned with the goats.

PRAYER.

O Lord, Thou hast shown me such an excess of bounty as to choose me from among so many others, to serve Thee in Thy own house with Thy most beloved servants. I know how great is that grace, and how unworthy of it I have been. Behold, I am willing to correspond to so great a love. I will obey Thee. Since Thou hast been towards me so liberal as to call me when I did not seek Thee, and when I was so ungrateful, permit it not that I should offer to Thee that greater excess of ingratitude, to embrace again my enemy, the world, in which heretofore I have so oftentimes forfeited Thy grace and my eternal salvation, and thus to forsake Thee, who hast shed Thy blood and given Thy life for my sake. Since Thou hast called me, give me also the strength to correspond to the call. Already have I promised to obey Thee. I promise it again, but without the grace of perseverance I cannot be faithful to Thee. This perseverance I ask from Thee, and through Thy own merits it is that I wish it and hope to obtain it. Give me the courage to vanquish the passions of the flesh, through which the devil seeks to induce me to betray Thee. I love Thee, O my Jesus, to Thee I consecrate myself entirely. I am already Thine, I will be always Thine. O Mary, my mother and my hope, thou art the mother of perseverance. This grace is only dispensed through thy hands; do thou obtain it for me. In thee do I confide.

CONSIDERATION IV.

The Torment which in Hell will be the Lot of him who is damned for having lost his Vocation.

The pain of having through one's own fault lost some great good, or of having brought upon one's self voluntarily some great evil, is a pain so great that even in this life it causes an insupportable torment. But what torment will that youth, called by the singular favor of God to the religious state, feel in hell when he then perceives that if he had obeyed God he would have attained a high place in paradise, and sees himself nevertheless confined in that prison of torments, without hope of remedy for this his eternal ruin! Their worm dieth not.

This will be that worm, which, living always, will always gnaw his heart by a continual remorse. He will say then, What a fool I was! I might have become a great saint. And if I had obeyed, I would certainly have become so; and now I am damned without remedy.

Miserable being! Then for his greater torment, on the day of judgment he will see and recognize at the right hand, and crowned as saints, those who have followed their vocation, and, leaving the world, have retired to the house of God, to which he also had been once called. And then will he see himself separated from the company of the blessed, and placed in the midst of that innumerable and miserable crew of the damned, for his disobedience to the voice of God.

We know well, as we have considered above, that to this most unhappy lot he exposes himself, who, in order to follow his own caprice, turns a deaf ear to the call of God. Therefore, my brother, you who have already been called to become a saint in the house of God, consider that you will expose yourself to a great danger should you lose your vocation through your own fault. Consider that this very vocation which God in his sovereign bounty has given you, in order, as it were, to take you out from among the populace and place you among the chosen princes of his paradise, will, through your own fault, should you be unfaithful to it, become an especial hell for you. Make your choice then, for God leaves it in your own hands, either to be a great king in paradise, or a reprobate in hell, more despairing than the rest.
Prayer.

No, my God, permit me not to disobey Thee and to be unfaithful. I see Thy goodness, and thank Thee for that instead of casting me away from Thy face, and banishing me into hell, as I have so often deserved, Thou callest me to become a saint, and prepares, for me a high place in paradise. I see that I should deserve a double torment, should I not correspond with this grace, which is not given to all. I will obey Thee. Behold, I am Thine, and always will be Thine. I embrace with joy all the pains and discomforts of the religious life, to which Thou invitest me. And what are these pains in comparison with the eternal pains, which I have deserved? I was entirely lost through my sins; now I give myself entirely to Thee. Dispose of me and my life as Thou pleasest. Accept, O Lord, of one already condemned to hell, as I have been, to serve Thee and love Thee in this life and in the next. I will love Thee as much as I have deserved to be doomed to hate Thee in hell, O God, worthy of an infinite love! O my Jesus! Thou hast broken those chains by which the world held me bound; Thou hast delivered me from the servitude of my enemies. I will love Thee much, then, O my love and for the love I bear Thee, I will always love Thee and obey Thee. Always will 1 thank Thee, O Mary, my advocate, who hast obtained this mercy for me. Help me, and suffer me not to be ungrateful to that God who has loved me so much. Obtain for me that I may die rather than be unfaithful to so great a grace. Thus I hope.

CONSIDERATION V.

The Immense Glory which Religious enjoy in Heaven.

Consider, in the first place, that which St. Bernard says, that it is difficult for religious who die in the religious state to be damned. "From the cell to heaven the way is easy; one scarcely ever descends from his cell into hell." And the reason which the saint adduces is, "Because one scarcely ever perseveres in it until death, unless he be predestinated." For a religious with difficulty perseveres until his death, if he be not of the number of the elect of paradise. Therefore, St. Laurence Justinian called the religious state the gate of

49

paradise. "Of that heavenly city this is the gate." And he said that "Therefore the religious have a great sign of their predestination."

Consider, moreover, that the reward of heaven, as the Apostle says, is "A crown of justice;" wherefore God, though he rewards us for our works more abundantly than we deserve, rewards us nevertheless in proportion to the works we have done. He will render to everyone according to his works. From this consider how exceedingly great will be the reward which God will give in heaven to good religious, in consideration of the great merits they daily acquire.

The religious gives to God all his goods of this earth, and is content to be entirely poor, without possessing anything. The religious renounces all attachment to his parents, friends, and country, in order to unite himself more closely to God. The religious continually mortifies himself in many things which he would enjoy in the world. The religious, finally, gives to God his whole self, by giving him his will through the vow of obedience.

But the dearest thing that we have is our own will, and what God, of all other things, requires of us most is our heart; that is to say, our will. My son, give Me thy heart. He who serves God in the world will give him his possessions, but not himself; he will give him a part and not the whole, for he will give him indeed his goods by alms–deeds, his food by fasting, his blood by disciplines, etc.; but he will always reserve for himself his own will, fasting when he pleases, praying when he likes. But the religious, giving him his own will, gives himself and gives all, gives not only the fruits of the tree, but the whole tree itself. Whence he may then truly say to him, O Lord, having given Thee my will, I have nothing more to give to Thee.

And, therefore, in all that he does through obedience he is sure to do the will of God perfectly, and merits by all, not only when he prays, when he hears confessions, when he preaches, or fasts, or practises other mortifications, but also when he takes his food, when he sweeps his room, when he makes his bed, when he takes his rest, when he recreates himself; for, doing all this through obedience, in all he does the will of God. St. Mary Magdalene de Pazzi said that all that is done through obedience is a prayer. Hence, St. Anselm, speaking of those who love obedience, asserted that all that religious do is meritorious for them. St. Aloysius Gonzaga said that in religion one sails, as it were, in a vessel, in which he even advances who does not row.

Oh, how much more will a religious gain in one month by observing his Rule than a secular, with all his penance and prayers, in a year! Of that disciple of Dorotheus called Dositheus, it was revealed that for the five years he had lived under obedience, there was given to him in heaven the glory of St. Paul the Hermit and of St. Anthony the Abbot, both of whom had, for so many years, lived in the desert. Religious, it is true, have to suffer the inconveniences of regular observance: Going, they went and wept. But when are they called to the other life, they will go to heaven, but, coming, they shall come with joyfulness, carrying their sheaves. Whence they shall then sing, The lines are fallen unto me in goodly places, for my inheritance is goodly to me. These bonds which have bound me to the Lord have become for me exceedingly precious, and the glory they have acquired for me is exceedingly great.

Prayer.

Is it possible, O my God and my true lover, that Thou desirest so much my good, and to be loved by me, and that I, miserable that I am, desire so little to love and to please Thee? For what end hast Thou favored me with so many graces, and taken me out of the world? O my Jesus! I understand Thee. Thou lovest me much, Thou wilt have me love Thee much also, and be all Thine, in this life and in the next. Thou wishest that my love should not be divided with creatures, but wilt have it be wholly for Thyself, the only good, the only lovely one, and worthy of infinite love. Ah, my Lord, my treasure, my love, my all, yet I pant and truly desire to love Thee, and to love no other but Thee. I thank Thee for this desire Thou hast given me; preserve it in me, always increase it in me, and grant that I may please Thee, and love Thee on this earth as Thou desirest, so that I may come hereafter to love Thee face to face, with all my strength in paradise. Behold, this is all that I ask from Thee. Thee will I love, O my God! I will love Thee, and for Thy love I offer myself to suffer every pain. I will become a saint, not that I may enjoy great delight in heaven, but to please Thee much, O my beloved Lord and to love Thee much forever. Graciously hear me, O eternal Father, for the love of Jesus Christ.

My Mother Mary, for the love of this thy Son, help thou me. Thou art my hope; from thee I hope every good.

CONSIDERATION VI.

The Interior Peace that God gives
Good Religious to Enjoy.

The promises of God cannot fail. God has said, Every one that has left house, or brethren, or sisters, or father, or mother, . . . or lands for My name's sake, shall receive an hundredfold, and shall possess life everlasting. That is, the hundredfold on thus earth, and life everlasting in heaven.

The peace of the soul is a good which is of greater value than all the kingdoms of the world. And what avails it to have the dominions of the whole world without interior peace? Better is it to be the poorest villager, and to be content, than to be the lord of the whole world, and to live a discontented life. But who can give this peace? The unquiet world? Oh no, peace is a good that is obtained only from God. "O God!" prays the Church, "Give to Thy servants that peace which the world cannot give." Therefore he is called the God of all consolation. But if God be the sole giver of peace, to whom shall we suppose will he give that peace but to those who leave all, and detach themselves from all creatures, in order to give themselves entirely to their Creator? And therefore is it seen that good religious shut up in their cells, though mortified, despised, and poor, live a more contented life than the great ones of the world, with all the riches, the pomps, and diversions they enjoy.

St. Scholastica said that if men knew the peace that good religious enjoy, the whole world would become a monastery; and St, Mary Magdalene of Pazzi said that all, if they knew it, would scale the walls of the monasteries, in order to get into them. The human heart having been created for an infinite good, all creatures cannot content it, they being finite, imperfect, and few; God alone, who is an infinite good, can render it content. Delight in the Lord and He will give thee the request of thy heart. Oh no; a good religious united with God envies none of the princes of the world who possess kingdoms, riches, and honors. "Let the rich," he will say with St. Paulinus, "Have their riches, the kings have their kingdoms, to me Christ is my kingdom and my glory." He will see those of the world foolishly glory in their displays and vanities; but he, seeking always to detach himself more from earthly things, always to unite himself more closely to his God, will live contented in this life, and will say, Some trust in chariots, and some in horses, but we will call upon the name of the Lord, our God.

St. Teresa said that one drop of heavenly consolation is of greater value than all the pleasures of the world. Father Charles of Lorraine, having become a religious, said that God, by one moment of the happiness that he gave him to feel in religion, super abundantly paid him for all he had left for God. Hence his joyfulness was sometimes so great that, when alone in his cell, he could not help beginning to leap. The Blessed Seraphino of Ascoli, a Capuchin lay–brother, said that he would not exchange a foot length of his cord for all the kingdoms of the world.

Oh, what contentment does, he find who, having left all for God, is able to say with St. Francis, "My God and my all!" And with that to see himself freed from the servitude of the world, from the thraldom of worldly fashion, and from all earthly affections. This is the liberty that is enjoyed by the children of God, such as good religious are. It is true that in the beginning, the deprivation of the conversations and pastimes of the world, the observances of the Community, and the rules, seem to be thorns; but these thorns, as our Lord said to St. Bridget, will all become flowers and delights to him who courageously bears their first sting, and he will taste on this earth that peace which, as St. Paul says, surpasseth all the gratifications of the senses, and all the enjoyments of feasts, of banquets, and of the pleasures of the world: The peace of God which surpasseth all understanding. And what greater peace can there be than to know that one pleases God?

Prayer.

O My Lord and my God, my all! I know that Thou alone canst make me contented in this and in the next life. But I will not love Thee for my own contentment, I will love Thee only to content Thy heart. I wish this to be my peace, my only satisfaction during my whole life, to unite my will to Thy holy will, even should I have to suffer every pain in order to do this. Thou art my God, I am Thy creature. And what can I hope for greater than to please Thee, my Lord, my God, who hast been so partial in Thy love towards me? Thou, O my Jesus, hast left heaven to live for the love of me—a poor and mortified life. I leave all to live only for the love of Thee, my most blessed Redeemer. I love Thee with my whole heart; if only Thou wilt give me the grace to love Thee, treat me as Thou pleasest.
O Mary, Mother of my God, protect me and render me like to thee, not in thy glory, which I do not deserve, as thou dost, but in pleasing God, and obeying his holy will, as thou didst.

CONSIDERATION VII.

The Damage done to Religious by Tepidity.

Consider the misery of that religious who, after having left his home, his parents, and the world with all its pleasures, and after having given himself to Jesus Christ, consecrating to him his will and his liberty, exposes himself at last

55

to the danger of being damned, by falling into a lukewarm and negligent life, and continuing in it. Oh, no; not far from perdition is a lukewarm religious, who has been called into the house of God to become a saint. God threatens to reject such, and to abandon them if they do not amend. But because thou art lukewarm, I will begin to vomit thee out of My mouth.

St. Ignatius of Loyola, seeing a lay–brother of his Order become lukewarm in the service of God, called him one day and said to him, Tell me, my brother, what did you come in religion to do? He answered, To serve God. O my brother, replied the saint, what have you said? If you had answered that you came to serve a cardinal, or a prince of this earth, you would be more excusable; but you say that you came to serve God, and do you serve him thus?

Father Nieremberg says that some are called by God to be saved only as saints, so that if they should not take care to live as saints, thinking to be saved as imperfect Christians, they will not be saved at all. And St. Augustine says that such are in most cases abandoned by God: "Negligent souls God is accustomed to abandon." And how does he abandon them? By permitting them from lighter faults, which they see and do not mind, to fall into grievous, ones, and to lose divine grace and their vocation. St. Teresa of Jesus saw the place prepared for her in hell, had she not detached herself from an earthly, though not a grievously culpable, affection. He that contemneth small things, shall fall by little and little.

Many wish to follow Jesus Christ, but from afar, as St. Peter did, who, when his Master was arrested in the garden, says St. Matthew, followed Him afar off. But by doing so that will easily happen to them which happened to St. Peter; namely, that, when the occasion came, he denied Jesus Christ. A lukewarm religious will be contented with what little he does for God; but God, who called him to a perfect life, will not be contented, and, in punishment for his ingratitude, will not only deprive him of his special favors, but will sometimes permit his fall. "When you said, It is enough, then you perished," says St. Augustine. The fig–tree of the Gospel was cast into the fire, only because it brought forth no fruit.

Father Louis de Ponte said, "I have committed many faults, but I have never made peace with them." Miserable is that religious who, being called to perfection, makes peace with his defects. As long as we detest our imperfections, there is hope that we may still become saints; but when we commit faults and make little of them, then, says St. Bernard, the hope of becoming saints is lost. He who soweth sparingly shall also reap sparingly. Common graces do not suffice to make one a saint; extraordinary ones are necessary. But how shall God be liberal with his favors towards that one who acts sparingly and with reserve in his love towards him?

Moreover, to become a saint, one must have courage and strength to overcome all repugnances; and let no one ever believe, says St. Bernard, that he will be able to attain to perfection if he does not render himself singular among others in the practice of virtue. "What is perfect cannot but be singular." Reflect, my brother, for what have you left the world and all? To become a saint. But that lukewarm and imperfect life which you lead, is that the way of becoming a saint? St. Teresa animated her daughters by saying to them, "My sisters, you have done the principal thing necessary to become saints; the least remains yet to be done." The same I say to you; you have, perhaps, done the chief part already;

you have left your country, your home, your parents, your goods, and your amusements; the least remains yet to be done, to become a saint; do it.

Prayer.

O my God, reject me not, as I deserve, for I will amend. I know well that so negligent a life as mine cannot satisfy Thee. I know that I have myself, by my lukewarmness, shut the door against the graces which Thou didst desire to bestow upon me. O Lord, do not yet abandon me, continue to be merciful towards me; I will rise from this miserable state. I will for the future be more careful to overcome my passions, to follow Thy inspirations, and never will I through slothfulness omit my duties, but I will fulfil them with greater diligence. In short, I will, from this time forward, do all I can to please Thee, and I will neglect nothing which I may know to be pleasing to Thee. Since thou, O my Jesus, hast been so liberal with Thy graces towards me, and hast deigned to give Thy blood and Thy life for me, there is no reason I should act with such reserve towards Thee. Thou art worthy of all honor, all love, and to please Thee one ought gladly to undergo every labor, every pain. But, O my Redeemer! Thou knowest my weakness, help me with Thy powerful grace; in Thee I confide. O immaculate Virgin Mary, thou who hast helped me to leave the world, help me to overcome myself and to become a saint.

CONSIDERATION VIII.

How Dear to God is a Soul that gives itself entirely to Him.

God loves all those who love him: I love them that love Me.

Many, however, give themselves to God, but preserve still in their hearts some attachment to creatures, which prevents them from belonging entirely to God. How, then, shall God give himself entirely to that one who, besides his God, loves creatures still? It is just that he should act with reserve towards those who act with reserve towards him. On the contrary, he gives himself entirely to those souls, who, driving from their hearts everything that is not God, and does not lead them to his love, and giving themselves to him without reserve, truly say to him, My God and my all. St. Teresa, as long as she entertained an inordinate affection, though not an impure one, could not hear from Jesus Christ what afterwards she heard, when, freeing herself from every attachment, she gave herself entirely to the divine love; namely, the Lord saying to her, "Now, because thou art all mine, I am all thine."

Consider that the Son of God has already given himself entirely to us: A child is born to us, and a son is given to us. He has given himself to us through the love he bears to us. He hath loved us, and hath delivered Himself for us. It is, then, just, says St. John Chrysostom, that when a God has given himself to you, without reserve,–"He has given thee all, nothing has he left to himself,"–you also should give yourself to God, without reserve; and that always henceforth, burning with divine love, you should sing to him:

Thine wholly always will I be;
Thou hast bestowed Thyself on me,
Wholly I give myself to Thee.

St. Teresa revealed to one of her nuns, appearing to her after her death, that God loves a soul that, as a spouse, gives itself entirely to him, more than a thousand tepid and imperfect ones. From these generous souls, given entirely to God, is the choir of Seraphim completed. The Lord himself says that he loves a soul that attends to its perfection, so much that he seems not to love any other. One is my dove, my perfect one is but one. Hence Blessed Giles exhorts us, "One for one," by which he wishes to say that this one soul we have we ought to give wholly, not divided, to that One who alone deserves all love, on whom depends all our good, and who loves us more than all. "Leave all and you shall find all," says Thomas à Kempis. Leave all for God, and in God you will find all. "O soul!" concludes St. Bernard, "Be alone, that you may keep yourself for him alone." Keep yourself alone, give no part of your affections to creatures, that you may belong alone to Him who alone deserves an infinite love, and whom alone you ought to love.

Prayer.

My beloved to me and I to him. As then, O my God! Thou hast given Thyself entirely to me, I should be too ungrateful if I should not give myself entirely to Thee; since Thou wouldst have me belong wholly to Thee, behold, O my Lord! I give myself entirely to Thee. Accept me through Thy mercy, disdain me not. Grant that this my heart, which once loved creatures, may turn now wholly to Thy infinite goodness. "Let me henceforth die," said St. Teresa, "Let another than myself live in me. Let God live in me, and give me life. Let him reign, and let me be his slave, for my soul wishes no other liberty." This my heart is too small, O God most worthy of love, and it is too little able to love Thee, who art deserving of an infinite love. I should then commit against Thee too great an injustice, should I still divide it by loving anything besides Thee. I love Thee, my God, above everything. I love only Thee; I renounce all creatures, and give myself entirely to Thee, my Jesus, my Saviour, my love, my all. I say, and always will say, What have I in heaven, and besides Thee, what do I desire on earth? . . . Thou art the God of my heart, and the God that is my portion forever. I desire nothing, either in this life or in the next, but to possess the treasure of Thy love. I am unwilling that creatures should have any more a place in my heart; Thou alone must be its master. To Thee only shall it belong for the future. Thou only shalt be my God, my repose, my desire, all my love, "Give me only Thy love and Thy grace, and I am rich enough." O most holy Virgin Mary, obtain for me this, that I may be faithful to God, and never recall the donation which I have made of myself to him.

CONSIDERATION IX.

How Necessary it is, in order to become a Saint, to have a Great Desire for such a Thing.

No saint has ever attained to sanctity without a great desire. As wings are necessary to birds in order to fly, so holy desires are necessary to the soul in order to advance in the road of perfection. To become a saint, we must detach ourselves from creatures, conquer our passions, overcome ourselves, and love crosses. But to do all this, much strength is required, and we must suffer much. But what is the effect of holy desire? St. Laurence Justinian answers us: "It supplies strength, and makes the pain easier to be borne." Hence the same saint adds that he has already vanquished who has a great desire of vanquishing. "A great part of the victory is the desire of vanquishing." He who wishes to reach the top of a high mountain will never reach it if he has not a great desire to do so. This will give him courage and strength to undergo the fatigue of ascending, otherwise he will stop at the foot, wearied and discouraged.

St. Bernard asserts that we acquire perfection in pro portion to the desire for it which we preserve in our heart. St. Teresa said that God loves generous souls that have great desires; for which reason the saint exhorted all in this way, "Let our thoughts be high. . . . for thence will come our good. We must not have low and little desires, but have that confidence in God that, if we make the proper efforts, we shall by little and little attain to that perfection which, with his grace, the saints have reached." In this way, the saints attained, in a short time, a great degree of perfection, and were able to do great things for God. Being made perfect in a short time, he fulfilled a long time. Thus St. Aloysius Gonzaga attained in a few years (he lived not over twenty−three years) such a degree of sanctity that St. Mary Magdalene of Pazzi, in an ecstasy, seeing him in heaven, said it seemed to her, in a certain way, that there was no saint in heaven who enjoyed a greater glory than Aloysius. She understood at the same time that he had arrived at so high a degree by the great desire he had cherished of being able to love God as much as he deserved, and that, seeing this beyond his reach, the holy youth had suffered on earth a martyrdom of love.

St. Bernard, being in religion, in order to excite his fervor, used to say to himself, "Bernard, for what did you come here?" I say the same to you: what have you come to do in the house of God? To become a saint? And what are you doing? Why do you lose the time? Tell me, do you desire to become a saint? If you do not, it is sure that you will never become one. If, then, you have not this desire, ask Jesus Christ for it; ask Mary for it; and if you have it, take courage, says St. Bernard, for many do not become saints, because they do not take courage. And so I repeat, let us take courage, and

great courage. What do we fear? What inspires this diffidence in us? That Lord, who has given us strength to leave
the world, will give us also the grace to embrace the life of a
saint. Everything comes to an end. Our life, be it a contented
or a discontented one, will also come to an end, but eternity
will never terminate. Only that little we have done for God
will console us in death and throughout eternity. The fatigue
will be short, eternal shall be the crown, which is already, so
to speak, before our eyes. How satisfied are the saints now
with all they have suffered for God! If a sorrow could enter
paradise, the Blessed would be sorry only for this, that they
have neglected to do for God what they might have done
more, but which now they are unable to do. Take courage,
then, and be prompt, for there is no time to lose; what can be
done to–day we may not be able to do tomorrow. St. Bernar-
dine of Sienna said that one moment of time is of as great
a value as God himself, for at every moment we may gain
God, his divine grace, and higher degrees of merits.

Prayer.

Behold, O my God, here I am. My heart is ready, O my God,
my heart is ready. See, I am prepared to do all that Thou
shalt require from me. O Lord, what wilt Thou have me to
do? Tell me, O Lord, what Thou desirest of me. I will obey
Thee in all. I am sorry for having lost so much time in which
I might have pleased Thee, and yet have not done so. I thank
Thee that still Thou givest me time to do it. Oh, no, I will not
lose any more time. I will and desire to become a saint, not
to obtain from Thee a greater glory and more delights. I will
become a saint, that I may love Thee more, and to please
Thee in this life and in the next. Make me, O Lord, to love
and please Thee as much as Thou desirest. Behold, this is
all I ask from Thee, O my God! I will love Thee, I will love

Thee; and, in order to love Thee, I offer myself to undergo every fatigue, and to suffer every pain. O my Lord, increase in me always this desire, and give me the grace to execute it. Of myself I can do nothing, but assisted by Thee I can do all. Eternal Father, for the love of Jesus Christ, graciously hear me. My Jesus, though the merits of Thy Passion, come to my succor. Or Mary, my hope, for the love of Jesus Christ, protect me.

CONSIDERATION X.

The Love we owe to Jesus Christ in consideration of the Love he has shown to us.

In order to understand the love which the Son of God has borne to us, it is enough to consider what St. Paul says of Jesus Christ: He emptied Himself , taking the form of a servant. . . . He humbled Himself, becoming obedient even to the death of the cross. "He emptied himself." O God, what admiration has it caused, and will it, through all eternity, cause to the angels to see a God who became man for the love of man, and submitted himself to all the weaknesses and sufferings of man! And the Word was made flesh. What a cause of astonishment would it not be to see a king become a worm for the sake of worms! But an infinitely greater wonder it is to see a God made man, and after this to see him humbled unto the painful and infamous death of the cross, on which he finished his most holy life.

Moses and Elias, on Mount Thabor, speaking of his death, as it is related in the Gospel, called it an excess: They spoke of His decease (the Latin word is "Excessus," which also means "Excess") that He should accomplish in Jerusalem. Yea, says Bonaventure, it is with reason the death of Jesus

Christ was called an excess, for it was an excess of suffering and of love, so much so that it would be impossible to believe it, if it had not already happened. It was truly an excess of love, adds St. Augustine, for to this end the Son of God wished to come on earth, to live a life so laborious and to die a death so bitter, namely, that he might make known to man how much he loved him. "Therefore Christ came, that man should know how much God loved him."

The Lord revealed to his servant Armella Nicolas that the love he bore to man was the cause of all his sufferings and of his death. If Jesus Christ had not been God, but only man and our friend, what greater love could he have shown us than to die for us? Greater love hath no man than this, that a man lay down his life for his friends. Ah, how, at the thought of the love shown us by Jesus Christ, the saints esteemed it little to give their life and their all for so loving a God! How many youths, how many noblemen, are there not, who have left their house, their country, their riches, their parents, and all, to retire into cloisters, to live only for the love of Jesus Christ! How many young virgins, renouncing their nuptials with princes and the great ones of the world, have gone with joyfulness to death, to render thus some compensation for the love of a God who had been executed on an infamous gibbet, and died for their sake!

This appeared to St. Mary Magdalene of Pazzi to be foolishness; hence she called her Jesus a fool of love. In exactly the same manner the Gentiles, as St. Paul attests, hearing the death of Jesus Christ preached to them, thought it foolishness not possible to be believed. We preach Christ crucified, unto the Jews indeed a stumbling- block, and unto the Gentiles foolishness. How is it possible, they said, that a God, most happy in himself, who is in want of nothing, should die for the sake of man, his servant? This would be as much as to believe that God became a fool for the love of men. Nevertheless, it is of faith that Jesus Christ, the true Son of God, did, for love of us, deliver himself up to death. He hath loved us, and hath delivered Himself for us. The same Mary Magdalene had reason then to exclaim, lamenting the ingratitude of men towards so loving a God, "O love not known! O love not loved!" Indeed, Jesus Christ is not loved by men, because they live in forgetfulness of his love.

And, in fact, a soul that considers a God who died for its sake, cannot live without loving him. The charity of Christ presseth us. The soul will feel itself inflamed, and as if constrained to love a God who has loved it so much. Jesus Christ could have saved us, says F. Nieremberg, with only one drop of his blood; but it was his will to shed all his blood, and to give his divine life, that at the sight of so many sufferings and of his death we might not content ourselves with an ordinary love, but be sweetly constrained to love with all our strength a God so full of love towards us. That they also who live may not live any more for themselves, but unto Him who died for them.

Prayer.

Indeed, O my Jesus, my Lord, and my Redeemer, only too much hast Thou obliged me to love Thee; too much my love has cost Thee. I should be too ungrateful if I should content myself to love with reserve a God who has given me his blood, his life, and his entire self. Oh, Thou hast died for me, Thy poor servant; it is but just that I should die for Thee, my God, and my all. Yes, O my Jesus! I detach myself from all, to give myself to Thee. I put away from me the love of all creatures, in order to consecrate myself entirely to Thy love. My helmed is chosen from among thousands. I choose

Thee alone out of all things for my good, my treasure, and my only love. I love Thee, O my love! I love Thee. Thou art not satisfied that I should love Thee a little only. Thou art not willing to have me love anything besides Thee. Thee I will please in all things, Thee will I love much; and Thou shalt be my only love. My God, my God, help me, that I may fully please Thee.

Mary, my queen, do thou also help me to love my God much. Amen. So I hope; so may it be.

CONSIDERATION XI.

The Great Happiness which Religious enjoy in dwelling in the same House with Jesus Christ in the Blessed Sacrament.

The Venerable Mother Mary of Jesus, foundress of a convent in Toulouse, said that she esteemed very much her lot as a religious, for two principal reasons. The first was, that religious, through the vow of obedience, belong entirely to God; and the second, that they have the privilege of dwelling always with Jesus Christ in the Blessed Sacrament. And in truth, if people of the world deem it so great a favor to be invited by kings, to dwell in their palaces; how much more favored should we esteem ourselves, who are admitted to dwell continually with the King of Heaven in his own house?

In houses of the religious, Jesus Christ dwells for their sake in the church, so that they can find him at all hours. Persons of the world can scarcely go to visit him during the day, and in many places only in the morning. But the religious finds him in the tabernacle, as often as he wishes, in the morning, in the afternoon, and during the night. There he may continually entertain himself with his Lord, and there Jesus Christ rejoices to converse familiarly with his beloved servants, whom, for this end, he has called out of Egypt, that he may be their companion during this life, hidden under the veil of the Most Holy Sacrament, and in the next unveiled in paradise. "O solitude," it may be said of every religious house, "In which God familiarly speaks and converses with his friends!" The souls that love Jesus Christ much do not know how to wish for any other paradise on this earth than to be in the presence of their Lord, who dwells in this sacrament for the love of those who seek and visit him.

His conversation hath no bitterness, nor His company any tediousness. He finds tediousness in the company of Jesus Christ, who does not love him. But those who on this earth have given all their love to Jesus Christ, find in the sacrament all their pleasure, their rest, their paradise, and therefore they keep their hearts always mindful to visit, as often as they can, their God in the sacrament, to pay their court to him, giving vent to their affections at the foot of the altar, offering him their afflictions, their desires of loving him, of seeing him face to face, and, in the mean time, of pleasing him in all things.

Prayer.

Behold me in Thy presence, O my Jesus, hidden in the sacrament, Thou art the self–same Jesus who for me didst sacrifice Thyself on the cross. Thou art he who lovest me so much, and who hast therefore confined Thyself in this prison of love. Amongst so many, who have offended Thee less than I, and who have loved Thee better than I, Thou hast chosen me, in Thy goodness, to keep Thee company in this house, where, having drawn me from the midst of the world, Thou hast destined me always to live united with Thee, and afterwards to have me nigh Thee to praise and to love Thee in Thy eternal kingdom. O Lord! I thank Thee. How have I deserved this happy lot? I have chosen to be an abject in the house of my God, rather than dwell in the tabernacles of sinners. Happy indeed am I, O my Jesus, to have left the world; and it is my great desire to perform the vilest office in Thy house rather than dwell in the proudest royal palaces of men. Receive me, then, O Lord, to stay with Thee all my life long; do not chase me away, as I deserve. Be pleased to allow that, among the many good brothers who serve Thee in this house, I, though I am a miserable sinner, may serve Thee also. Many years already have I lived far from Thee. But now that Thou hast enlightened me to know the vanity of the world, and my own foolishness, I will not depart any more from Thy feet, O my Jesus! Thy presence shall animate me to fight when I am tempted. The nearness of Thy abode shall remind me of the obligation I am under to love Thee, and always to have recourse to Thee in my combats against hell. I will always keep near to Thee, that I may unite myself to Thee, and attach myself closer to Thee. I love Thee, O my God, hidden in this sacrament. Thou, for the love of me, remainest always on this altar. I, for the love of Thee, will always remain in Thy presence as much as I shall be able. There enclosed Thou always lovest me, and here enclosed I will always love Thee. Always, then, O my Jesus, my love, my all, shall we remain together,—in time in this house, and during eternity, in paradise. This is my hope, so may it be. Most holy Mary, obtain for me a greater love for the Most Holy Sacrament.

CONSIDERATION XII.

The Life of Religious resembles mostly the Life of Jesus Christ.

The Apostle says that the eternal Father predestines to the kingdom of heaven those only who live conformably to the life, of the incarnate Word. Whom He foreknew, He also predestinated to be made conformable to the image of His Son. How happy, then, and secure of paradise should not religious be, seeing that God has called them to a state of life which of all other states is the most conformed to the life of Jesus Christ.

Jesus, on this earth, wished to live poor as the son and help-mate of a mechanic, in a poor dwelling, with poor clothing and poor food: Being rich, He became poor for your sake, that through His poverty you might become rich. Moreover, he chose a life the most entirely mortified, far from the delights of the world, and always full of pain and sorrow, from his birth to his death; hence by the prophet he was called The man of sorrows. By this he wished to give his servants to understand what ought to be the life of those who wish to follow him: If any man will come after Me, let him deny himself, take up his cross, and follow Me. According to this example, and to this invitation of Jesus Christ, the saints have endeavored to dispossess themselves of all earthly goods, and to load themselves with pains and crosses, in order thus to follow Christ, their beloved Lord.

Thus acted St. Benedict, who, being the son of the lord of Norcia, and a relative of the Emperor Justinian, and born amidst the riches and the pleasures of the world, while yet a youth of only fourteen years, went to live in a cavern on

70

Mount Sublaco, where he received no other sustenance but a piece of bread brought him every day as an alms by the hermit Romanus.

So acted St. Francis of Assisi, who renounced in favor of his father the whole lawful portion of his inheritance, even to the shirt he had on his back, and, thus poor and mortified, consecrated himself to Jesus Christ. Thus St. Francis Borgia, St. Aloysius Gonzaga, the one being Duke of Candia, the other of Castiglione, left all their riches, their estates, their vassals, their country, their house, their parents, and went to live a poor life in religion.

So have done so many other noblemen and princes even of royal blood. Blessed Zedmerra, daughter of the King of Ethiopia, renounced the kingdom to become a Dominican nun. Blessed Johanna of Portugal renounced the kingdom of France and England, to become a nun. In the Benedictine Order alone, there are found twenty–five emperors, and seventy-five kings and queens, who left the world to live poor, mortified, and forgotten by the world, in a poor cloister. Ah, indeed, these and not the grandees of the world, are the truly fortunate ones.

At present, worldlings think these to be fools, but in the valley of Josaphat they shall know that they themselves have been the fools; and when they see the saints on their thrones crowned by God, they shall say, lamenting and in despair, These are they whom we had sometime in derision, . . . we fools esteemed their life madness, but now they are numbered among the children of God, as their lot is among the saints.

Prayer.

Ah, my Master, and my Redeemer, Jesus, I am then of the number of those fortunate ones whom Thou hast called to follow Thee. O my Lord! I thank Thee for this. I leave all; would that I had more to leave, that I might draw near to Thee, my king and my God, who for the love of me, and to give me courage by Thy example, hast chosen for Thyself a life so poor and so painful. Walk on, O Lord, I will follow Thee. Choose Thou for me what cross Thou wilt, and help me. I will always carry it with constancy and love. I regret that for the past I have abandoned Thee, to follow my lusts and the vanities of the world; but now I will leave Thee no more. Bind me to Thy cross, and if through weakness I sometimes resist, draw me by the sweet bonds of Thy love. Suffer it not that I should ever leave Thee again. Yes, my Jesus, I renounce all the satisfactions of the world; my only satisfaction shall be to continue to love Thee, and to suffer all that pleases Thee. I hope thus to come myself one day in Thy kingdom, to be united with Thee by that bond of eternal love, where, loving Thee in Thy revealed glory, I need no more fear to be loosed and separated from Thee. I love Thee, O my God, my all and will always love Thee. Behold my hope, O Most Holy Mary, thou who, because the most conformed to Jesus, art now the nicest powerful to obtain this grace. Be thou my protectress!

CONSIDERATION XIII.

The Zeal which Religious ought to have for the Salvation of Souls.

He who is called to the Congregation of the Most Holy Redeemer will never be a true follower of Jesus Christ, and will never become a saint, if he fulfils not the end of his vocation, and has not the spirit of the Institute, which is the salvation of souls, and of those souls that are the most destitute of spiritual succor, such as the poor people in the country.

This was truly the end for which our Redeemer came down from heaven, who protests, The spirit of the Lord . . . hath anointed me to preach the Gospel to the poor. He sought no other proof of Peter's love for him but this, that he should procure the salvation of souls: Simon, son of John, lovest thou me? . . . Feed my sheep. He did not impose upon him, says St. John Chrysostom, penance, prayers, or other things, but only that he should endeavor to save his sheep: "Christ said not to him, throw your money away, practise fasting, fatigue your body with hard work, but he said, Feed my sheep." And he declares that he would look upon every benefit conferred on the least of our neighbors as conferred on himself. Amen, I say to you, since you have done it unto one of these my least brethren, you have done it unto we.

Every religious ought, therefore, with the utmost care, to entertain within himself this zeal, and this spirit of helping souls. To this end everyone ought to direct his studies, and when he shall afterwards have been assigned to his work by his Superiors, he ought to give to it all his thoughts, and his whole attention. He could not call himself a true brother of this Congregation, who, through the desire of attending only to himself and of leading a retired and solitary life, would not accept with all affection such an employment, when imposed on him by obedience.

What greater glory can a man have than to be, as St. Paul says, a co-operator with God in this great work of the salvation of souls? He who loves the Lord ardently is not content

73

to be alone in loving him, he would draw all to his love, saying with David, O magnify the Lord with me, and let us extol his name together. Hence St. Augustine exhorts all those who love God, "If you love God, draw all men to his love."

A good ground to hope for his own salvation has he who with true zeal labors for the salvation of souls. "Have you saved a soul," says St. Augustine, "Then you have predestinated your own." The Holy Ghost promises us, When thou shalt have labored for the welfare of a poor man, and by thy labor shalt have filled him (with divine grace), the Lord will fill thee with light and peace. In this—namely, in procuring the salvation of others—St. Paul placed his hope of eternal salvation, when he said to his disciples of Thessalonica, For what is our hope, or joy, or crown of glory? Are not you, in the presence of our Lord Jesus Christ at his coming?

Prayer.

O my Lord Jesus Christ, how can I thank Thee enough, since Thou hast called me to the same work that Thou didst Thyself on earth; namely, to go with my poor exertions and help souls to their salvation? How have I deserved this honor and this reward, after having offended Thee so grievously, and been the cause to others also of offending Thee? Yes, O my Lord! Thou callest me to help Thee in this great undertaking. I will serve Thee with all my strength. Behold, I offer Thee all my labor, and even my blood, in order to obey Thee. Nor do I by this aspire to satisfy my own inclination, or to gain applause and esteem from men; I desire nothing but to see Thee loved by all as Thou deservest. I prize my happy lot, and call myself fortunate, that Thou hast chosen me for this great work, in which I protest that I will renounce all praises of men and all self– satisfaction, and will only seek Thy glory. To Thee be all the honor and satisfaction, and to me only the discomforts, the blame, and the reproaches. Accept, O Lord, this offering, which I, a miserable sinner, who wish to love Thee and to see Thee loved by others, make of myself to thee, and give me strength to execute it.

Most Holy Mary, my advocate, who lovest souls so much, help me.

CONSIDERATION XIV.

How Necessary to Religious are the Virtues of Meekness and Humility.

Our most lovely Redeemer Jesus willed to be called a lamb, for the very reason that he might show us how meek and humble he was himself. These were the virtues which he principally wished his followers should learn from him: Learn from me, because I am meek and humble of heart. And these virtues he principally requires of religious who profess to imitate his most holy life.

He who lives as a solitary in a desert has not so much need of these virtues; but for him who lives in a Community, it is impossible not to meet, now and then, with a reprimand from his Superiors, or something disagreeable from his companions. In such cases, a religious who loves not meekness will commit a thousand faults every day, and live an unquiet life. He must be all sweetness with everybody,—with strangers, with companions, and also with inferiors if he should ever be come Superior; and if he be an inferior, he must consider that one act of meekness in bearing contempt and reproach is of greater value to him than a thousand fasts and a thousand disciplines.

St. Francis said that many make their perfection consist in exterior mortifications, and, after all, are not able to bear one injurious word. "Not understanding," he added, "How much greater gain is made by patiently bearing injuries." How many persons, as St. Bernard remarks, are all sweetness when nothing is said or done contrary to their inclination, but show their want of meekness when anything crosses them! And if anyone should ever be Superior, let him believe that one reprimand made with meekness will profit his subjects more than a thousand made with severity. The meek are useful to themselves and to others, as St. John Chrysostom teaches. In short, as the same saint said, the greatest sign of a virtuous soul is to see it meek on occasions of contradiction. A meek heart is the pleasure of the heart of God. That which is agreeable to him is faith and meekness. It would be well for a religious to represent to himself, in his meditations, all the contrarieties that may happen to him, and thus arm himself against them; and then, when the occasion happens, he ought to do violence to himself, that he may not be excited and break out in impatience. Therefore, he should refrain from speaking when his mind is disturbed, till he is certain that he has become calm again.

But to bear injuries quietly, it is above all necessary to have a great fund of humility. He who is truly humble is not only unmoved when he sees himself despised, but is even pleased, and rejoices at it in his spirit, however the flesh may resent it; for he sees himself treated as he deserves, and made conformable to Jesus Christ, who, worthy as he was of every honor, chose, for the love of us, to be satiated with contempt and injuries. Brother Juniper, a disciple of St. Francis, when an injury was done to him, held up his cowl, as if lie expected to receive pearls falling from heaven. The saints have been more desirous of injuries than worldlings are covetous of applause and honor. And of what use is a religious who does not know how to bear contempt for God's sake? He is always proud, and only humble in name and a hypocrite, whom divine grace will repulse, as the Holy Ghost says: God resisteth the proud, but to the humble he giveth grace.

Prayer.

O my most humble Jesus, who, for the love of me, didst humble Thyself, and become obedient unto the death of the cross, how have I the courage to appear before Thee, and call myself Thy follower, for I see myself to be such a sinner and so proud that I cannot bear a single injury without resenting it. Whence can come such pride in me, who for my sins have so many times deserved to be cast forever into hell with the devils? Ah, my despised Jesus, help me and make me conformable to Thee. I will change my life. Thou, for love of me, hast borne so much contempt; I, for love of Thee, will bear every injury. Thou, O my Redeemer, hast rendered contempt too honorable and desirable, since Thou hast embraced it with so much love, during Thy own life, far be it from me to glory but in the cross of our Lord Jesus Christ. O my most humble mistress Mary, mother of God, thou who wast in all, and especially in suffering, the most conformed to thy Son, obtain for me the grace to bear in peace all injuries which henceforward shall be offered to me. Amen.

CONSIDERATION XV.

How much Religious ought to confide in the Patronage of Mary.

If it is true, and most true it is, that, according to the saying of St. Peter Damian, the divine mother, the most holy Mary, loves all men with such an affection that after God there is not, nor can there be, anyone who surpasses or equals her in her love,–"She loves us with an invincible love,"–how much must we think this great queen loves religious, who have consecrated their liberty, their life, and their all to the love of Jesus Christ? She sees well enough that the life of such as these is more conformable to her own life, and to that of her divine Son; she sees them often occupied in praising her, and continually attentive to honor her by their novenas, visits, rosaries, fasts, etc. She beholds them often at her feet, intent on invoking her aid, asking graces of her, and graces all con-formed to her holy desires; that is, the grace of perseverance in the divine service, of strength in their temptations, of de-tachment from this world, and of love towards God, Ah, how can we doubt that she employs all her power and her mercy for the benefit of religious, and especially of those who be-long to this holy Congregation of the Most Holy Redeemer in which, as it is well known, we make special profession of honoring the Virgin Mother by visits, by fasting on Satur-days, by special mortifications during her novenas, etc., and by everywhere promoting devotion to her by sermons and novenas in her honor!

She, the great mistress, is grateful. I love those who love Me. Yes, she is so grateful that, as St. Andrew of Crete says, "To him who does her the least service she is accustomed to return great favors." She promises liberally those who love her, and who promote her honor among others, to deliver them from sin: "Those that work by me shall not sin." She also promises to them paradise: "Those that explain me shall have life everlasting."

For which reason we especially ought to thank God for having called us to this Congregation, where by the usages of the Community and the example of our companions, we are often reminded, and in some way constrained, to have recourse to Mary, and continually to honor this our most loving mother, who is called, and is, the joy, the hope, the life, and the salvation of those who invoke and honor her.

Prayer.

My most beloved, most lovely, and most loving queen, I always thank my Lord and thee, who hast not only drawn me, out of the world, but also called me to live in this Congregation, where a special devotion is practised to thee. Accept of me then, my mother, to serve thee. Among so many of thy beloved sons, do not scorn to let me serve thee also, miserable though I am. Thou after God shalt always be my hope and my love. In all my wants, in all my tribulations and temptations, I will always have recourse to thee; thou shalt be my refuge, my consolation. I am unwilling that anyone except God and thee should comfort me in my combats, in the sadness and the tediousness of this life. For thy service I renounce all the kingdoms of the whole world. My kingdom on this earth shall be to serve, bless, and love thee, O my most lovely mistress! "Whom to serve is to reign," as St. Anselm says. Thou art the mother, of perseverance; obtain for me to be faithful to thee until death. By so doing I hope, and firmly hope, one day to come where thou reignest, to praise and bless thee forever, to depart no more from thy holy feet. Jesus and Mary, I protest, with your loving servant Alphonsus Rodriguez, "My most sweet loves, let me suffer for you, let me die for you, let me be all yours, and not at all my own."

Prayer.

(Taken from St. Thomas of Aquinas.)

Grant me, O my God, to know Thy will, and to accomplish it perfectly to Thy glory. Give me the strength not to fail in prosperity, so as to exalt myself presumptuously; not to fail in adversity, so as to be cast down by it. Let me feel joy or sorrow at nothing else, but what leads me to Thee, or separates me from Thee. Let me desire to please none, let me fear to displease none, but Thee Let all the goods of the world be vile to me, and all Thy gifts dear to me, for the love of Thee, and be Thou dear to me above everything. Let all joy without Thee be tediousness to me, and let every fatigue which is for Thee be pleasing to me, so that outside of Thee I may wish for nothing. Grant that to Thee I may always direct all my thoughts and all my affections. Make me, O Lord, obedient without reply, poor without desire, chaste without defilement, patient without murmur, humble without simulation, joyous without dissipation, fearful without diffidence, diligent without solicitude, prudent without duplicity. Grant me the ability to do good without presumption, to reprove without becoming haughty, to edify my neighbor by my example without dissimulation. Give me a watchful heart, that vain thoughts may not carry me away from Thee; a noble heart, that is not bowed down by unworthy affections; a right heart, that is not moved by perverse intentions; a heart strong in tribulations; a heart free from earthly attachment. Give me to be enlightened in knowing Thee, diligent in seeking Thee, wise in finding Thee, persevering in pleasing Thee, grateful in thanking Thee. Finally, give me strength in this life to embrace every punishment due to my sins, and then, in the next, the grace forever to see Thee, possess Thee, and love Thee, face to face. Amen.

O Mary, my queen, my hope, and my mother! I love thee, I confide in thee. I beseech thee by the love of Jesus, by the joy thou didst feel in becoming his mother, and by the sorrow thou didst feel at his death, obtain of God for me a great sorrow for my sins and the pardon of them, perseverance in a good life, a pure love towards God with a perfect conformity to his holy will. Thou art the refuge of sinners, thou art then my refuge. To thee I recommend my soul and my eternal salvation. Receive me as thy servant, and as such protect me always, and especially at the time of my death. Thou with thy powerful intercession must save me; this is my hope, thus may it be!

ANSWER TO A YOUNG MAN WHO ASKS
COUNSEL ON THE CHOICE OF A STATE OF LIFE.

I read in your letter that some time ago you felt inspired by God to become a religious, and that after wards many doubts arose in your mind, and especially this one, that, without becoming a religious, you might sanctify yourself also in the world.

I will answer your letter briefly, for, should you wish to read something more complete, you can read a little work of mine, which has already been printed, under the title "Counsels concerning Religious Vocation," in which I have treated this matter more fully. Here I will only say, briefly, that this point of the choice of a state of life is of the greatest importance, as upon it depends our eternal salvation. He who chooses the state to which God calls him will save himself with facility, and for him who does not obey the divine call it will be difficult—yes, morally impossible—to save himself. The greatest number of those who are damned, are damned for not having corresponded to the call of God.

In order, therefore, that you may be able to choose that state, which will be the surest for attaining eternal salvation, consider that your soul is immortal, and that the only end for which God has placed you in this world was, not certainly that you may acquire money and honors on this earth, and thus live a comfortable and delightful life, but that by holy virtues you may merit eternal life. In the day of judgment it will avail you nothing to have advanced your family, and to have made a figure in the world; it will only avail you to have served and loved Jesus Christ, who is to be your judge. You have a thought which tells you that you will also be able to sanctify yourself by remaining in the world. Yes, my dear sir, you will be able, but it is difficult, and if you are truly called by God to the religious state, and yet remain in the world, it is, as I have said above, morally impossible, because those helps will be denied you which God had prepared for you in religion, and without them you will not save yourself. To sanctify yourself it is necessary for you to employ the means,–such as, to avoid evil occasions, to remain detached from earthly goods, to live a life recollected in God; and to maintain this, it is necessary to receive the sacraments frequently, to make your meditation, your spiritual reading, and to perform other devout exercises, every day, otherwise it is impossible to preserve the spirit of fervor. Now, it is difficult, not to say impossible, to practise all this in the midst of the noise and the disturbances of the world; for family affairs, the necessities of the house, the complaints of parents, the quarrels and persecutions with which the world is so full, will keep your mind so occupied by cares and fears that you will barely be able in the evening to recommend yourself to God, and even this will be done with many distractions. You would wish to make your meditation, to read spiritual books, to receive Holy Communion often, to visit every day the Sacrament of the altar; but from all this you will be prevented by the affairs of the world, and the little you do will be imperfect, because it is done in the midst of a thousand distractions, and with coldness of heart. Your life will thus be always unquiet, and your death more unquiet still.

On one side, worldly friends will not fail to inspire you with a fear of embracing the religious life, as being a hard life and full of troubles. On the Other, the world offers you amusements, money, and a contented life. Reflect well, and do not allow yourself to be led into error. Be persuaded that the world is a traitor that makes promises and does not care about the fulfilment of them. It offers you indeed all these earthly things, but suppose it should give them to you, could it also give you peace of soul? No, God only can give true peace. The soul is created only for God, to love him in this life and to enjoy him in the next, and therefore God only can content it. All the pleasures and riches of the earth cannot give true peace; nay, those who in this life abound the most with such goods are the most troubled and afflicted, as Solomon confesses who had them in abundance. All, says he, is vanity and affliction of spirit. 1 If the world, with its goods, could make us happy, the rich, the great, the monarchs, who are in no want of wealth, honors, and amusements, would be fully contented. But experience shows how it is with these mighty ones of the earth; the greater they are, the greater are the vexations, fears, and afflictions they have to suffer. A poor Capuchin lay–brother, who goes about girded with a cord over a sackcloth, who lives on beans, and sleeps in a small cell on a little straw, is more contented than a prince with all his gilded trappings and riches, who has every day a sumptuous table, and who goes half sick to bed under a rich canopy, unable to sleep on account of the anguish which drives sleep away. He is a fool who loves the world and not God, said St. Philip Neri; and if these worldlings live such an unquiet life, much more unquiet still will be their death, when the priest, at their side, will intimate to them that they are about to be chased away from this world, saying: "Depart hence, Christian soul, from this world. Embrace the crucifix, for this world is at an end for you." The misery is, that in the world they think little of God, and just as little of the next life, where they must remain forever. All, or almost all, their thoughts are given to the things of this earth, and this is the cause that their life is so unhappy, and their death still more.

Nevertheless, that you may ascertain what state you ought to embrace, imagine yourself at the point of death, and choose that one which you would then wish to have chosen. Should you have erred, by neglecting the divine call, in order to follow your own inclinations, and to live with more liberty, there will then be no longer time to remedy the error. Consider that everything here below will come to an end. The fashion of this world passeth away. The scenes of this world must finish for each one of us. Everything passes, and death draws near, and at every step we take we approach nearer to it, and, through death, nearer to eternity. For this we are born. Man shall go into the house of his eternity. Death will be upon us when we least think of it. Alas, when death draws near, what will then appear all the goods of this world, but the unreal pageantry of a theatre,—vanities, lies, and foolishness? And what profit will it then be, as Jesus Christ warns us, if we should have gained the whole world and lost our souls? It will help us only to die an unhappy death.

On the contrary, a young man who has left the world to give himself entirely to Jesus Christ, how contented will he feel, as he passes his days in the solitude of his cell, far from the tumult of the world and the dangers of losing God, which are in the world! In the monastery he will not have the entertainments of music, theatres, and balls, but he will have God to console him and to make him enjoy peace. I mean all that peace which is possible in this valley of tears, into which everyone is sent to suffer, and to merit by his patience that full peace which is prepared for him in heaven. But in this life even, far from the pastimes of the world, one loving look cast from time to time on the crucifix, one "Deus meus, et omnia," pronounced with affection, one "my God" said with a sigh of love, will console him more than all the pastimes and feasts of the world, which leave only bitterness behind them.

And if he lives content in such a life, more content will
he be still at his death at having chosen the religious state.
How much will it then console him to have spent his life
in prayer, in spiritual reading, in mortification, and in other
exercises of devotion, especially if he has been in an Order
employed in saving souls by preaching and hearing confessions,–things which at his death will all increase his confidence in Jesus Christ, who is truly grateful and liberal in
rewarding those who have labored for his glory!

But let us come to a conclusion with regard to your vocation.
Since the Lord has called you to leave the world, and to be
entirely his in religion, I tell you: Rejoice and tremble at the
same time. Rejoice, on one hand, and always thank the Lord,
because to be called by God to a perfect life is a grace which
he does not give to all. On the other hand, tremble, because
if you do not follow the divine call, you will put your eternal
salvation in great danger. It is not my intention here to relate
to you the many examples of young men who, because they
made no account of their vocation, have lived a miserable
life and died a horrible death. Hold for certain that, as God
has called you, you will never have peace, if you remain in
the world; and at your death you will be very unquiet, on
account of the remorse that then will torment you, for having
neglected to obey God, who had called you to the religious
state.

At the end of your letter you express a wish to learn from
me whether, in case you should not have the courage to enter
religion, it would be better to marry, as your parents wish,
or to become a secular priest. I answer: The married state I
cannot recommend to you, because St. Paul does not counsel

it to any one, except there be a necessity for it, arising out of habitual incontinence, which necessity, I hold for certain, does not exist in your case.

With regard, then, to the state of a secular priest, take notice that a secular priest has on him all the obligations of a priest, and all the distractions and dangers of a layman; for, living in the midst of the world, he cannot avoid the troubles which arise from his own household and from his parents, and cannot be free from the dangers to which his soul is exposed. He will have temptations in his own house, being unable to exclude women from it, whether relatives or servants, nor prevent other strangers from coming to see them. You should then stay there altogether retired in a separate room, and attend only to divine things. Now, this it is very difficult to practise; and therefore small, and very small, is the number of those priests who attend to their perfection in their own houses.

On the contrary, entering a monastery of strict observance, you will be freed from the disagreeable duty of thinking about your food and clothing, because there the Order provides you with all, there you will not have your parents to come and continually trouble you with all the disturbances that happen in their house; there no women enter to disturb your mind; and thus, far from the tumult of the world, you will have no one to hinder you in your prayers and your recollection.

I have said a monastery of strict observance; because if you want to enter another, where they live more freely, it is better for you to stay at home and attend there to the salvation of your soul as well as you can; for entering an Order where the spirit is relaxed, you expose yourself to the danger of being lost. Though you should enter with the resolution to attend to prayer and to the things of God only, yet, carried along by the bad example of your companions, .and seeing yourself derided and even persecuted, if you do not live as they do, you will leave off all your devotions, and do as the others do, as experience shows it to be commonly the case. But should God give you the grace of vocation, be careful to preserve it, by recommending yourself often to Jesus and Mary in holy prayer. I know that if you resolve to give yourself entirely to God, the devil from that moment will increase his efforts to tempt you to fall into sin, and especially to make you entirely his, and to remain his.

I conclude by offering you the assurance of my respectful consideration; I pray the Lord to make you belong entirely to himself, and remain, etc.

ADVICE TO A YOUNG PERSON IN DOUBT ABOUT THE STATE OF LIFE WHICH SHE OUGHT TO EMBRACE

My dear Sister in Jesus Christ:

You are deliberating about the choice of a state of life. I see that you are agitated because the world wishes you to belong to itself, and to enter the married state; and, on the other hand, Jesus Christ wishes you to give yourself to him by becoming a nun in some convent of exact observance.

Remember that on the choice which you make your eternal salvation will depend. Hence, I recommend you, as soon as you read this advice, to implore the Lord, every day, to give you light and strength to embrace that state which will be most conducive to your salvation; that thus you may not afterwards, when your error is irreparable, have to repent of the choice you have made for your whole life, and for all eternity.

Examine whether you will be more happy in having for your spouse a man of the world, or Jesus Christ, the Son of God and the King of heaven; see which of them appears to you the better spouse, and then make your choice. At the age of thirteen, the holy virgin St. Agnes was, on account of her extraordinary beauty, sought after by many. Among the rest, the son of the Roman Prefect asked her for his spouse; but looking at Jesus Christ, who wished her to belong to him, she said, I have found a spouse better than you and all the monarchs of this world; therefore I cannot exchange him for any other. And rather than exchange him she was content to lose her life, and cheerfully suffered martyrdom for Jesus Christ. The holy virgin Domitilla gave a similar answer to the Count Aurelian; she, too, died a martyr, and was burned alive, because she would not forsake Jesus Christ. Oh, how happy do these holy virgins now feel in heaven, how happy will they feel for all eternity, at having made so good a choice! The same happy lot awaits you, and will await all young persons who renounce the world in order to give themselves to Jesus Christ.

In the next place, examine the consequences of the state of the person who chooses the world, and of the person who makes choice of Jesus Christ. The world offers earthly goods, riches, honors, amusements, and pleasures. On the other hand, Jesus Christ presents to you scourges, thorns, opprobrium, and crosses; for these were the goods which he chose for himself all the days of his mortal life. But then he offers you two immense advantages which the world cannot give—peace of soul in this life, and paradise in the next.

Moreover, before you decide on embracing any state, you must reflect that your soul is immortal; that is, that after the present life which will soon end, you must pass into eternity, in which you will receive that place of punishment or of reward which you will have merited by your works during life. Thus, you must remain for all eternity in the house either of eternal life or of eternal death, in which, after your departure from this world, it will be your lot first to dwell: you will be either forever saved and happy amid the joys of paradise, or forever lost and in despair in the torments of hell. In the mean time, consider that everything in this world must soon end. Happy all that are saved; miserable the soul that is damned. Keep always in mind that great maxim of Jesus Christ: "What will it profit a man to gain the whole world if he lose his own soul?" This maxim has sent so many from the world to shut themselves up in the cloister, or to live in the deserts; it has inspired so many young persons with courage to forsake the world in order to give themselves to God and to die a holy death.

On the other hand, consider the unhappy lot of so many ladies of fortune, so many princesses and queens, who in the world have been attended, praised, honored, and almost adored; but if they are damned, what do they now find in hell of so much riches, of so many pleasures, of so many honors enjoyed in this life, but pains and remorse of conscience, which will torment them forever, as long as God shall be God, without any hope of remedy for their eternal ruin.

But let us now cast a glance at the goods which the world gives in this life to its followers, and to the goods which God gives to her who loves him and forsakes the world for his sake. The world makes great promises; but do we not all see that the world is a traitor that promises what it never performs? But though it should fulfil all its promises, what does it give? It gives earthly goods, but does it give the peace and the life of happiness which it promises? All its goods delight the senses and the flesh, but do not content the heart and the soul. Our souls have been created by God for the sole purpose of loving him in this life, and of enjoying him in the next. Hence, all the goods of the earth, all its delights, and all its grandeurs, are outside the heart; they enter not into the soul, which God only can content. Solomon has even called all worldly goods vanities and lies, which do not content but rather afflict the soul. Vanity of vanities and affliction of spirit. This we know also from experience, for we see that the more a person abounds in these goods, the greater her anguish and misery of mind. If by its good the world gave content to the soul, great indeed should be the happiness of princesses and queens, who want neither amusements, nor comedies, nor festivities, nor banquets, nor splendid palaces, nor beautiful carriages, nor costly dresses, nor precious jewels, nor servants, nor ladies of honor to attend and pay homage to them. But no; they who imagine them to be happy are deceived. Ask them whether they enjoy perfect peace, if they are perfectly content, and they will answer: What peace? What content? They will tell you that they lead a life of misery, and that they know not what peace is. The maltreatment which they receive from their husbands, the displeasure caused by their children, the wants of the house, the jealousies and fears to which they are subject, make them live in the midst of continual anguish and bitterness. Married women may be called martyrs of patience, if they bear all with resignation; but unless they are patient and resigned, they will suffer a martyrdom in this world, and a more painful martyrdom in the next.

The remorse of conscience, though they had nothing else to suffer, keeps married persons in continual torment. Being attached to earthly goods, they reflect but little on spiritual things; they seldom approach the sacraments, and seldom recommend themselves to God; and, being deprived of these helps to a good life, they will scarcely be able to live without sin, and without continual remorse of conscience. Behold, then, how all the joys promised by the world become to married per sons sources of bitterness, of fears, and of damnation. How many of them will say, Unhappy me, what will become of me after so many sins, after the life which I led, at a distance from God, always going from bad to worse? I would wish for retirement in order to spend a little time in mental prayer, but the affairs of the family and of the house, which is always in confusion, do not permit this. I would wish to hear sermons, to go to confession, to communicate often; I would wish to go often to the church, but my husband does not wish it. My unceasing occupations, the care of children, the frequent visits of friends, keep me confined to the house; and thus it is not without some difficulty that I can hear Mass at a late hour on festivals. How great was my folly in entering the married state, when I could become a saint in a convent! But all these lamentations only serve to increase their pain; because they see that it is no longer in their power to change the unhappy choice they have made of living in the world. And if their life is unhappy, their death will be much more miserable. At that awful hour they will be surrounded by servants, by their husbands, and children, bathed in tears; but instead of giving them relief, all these will be to them an occasion of greater affliction. And thus afflicted, poor in merits, and full of fears for their eternal salvation, they must go to present themselves to Jesus Christ to be judged by him. But, on the other hand, how great will be the happiness which a nun who has left the world for Jesus Christ will enjoy, living among so many spouses of God, and in a solitary cell, at a distance from the turmoils of the world, and from the continual and proximate danger of losing God, to which seculars are exposed. How much greater will be her consolation at death, after having spent her years in meditations, mortifications, and in so many spiritual exercises; in visits to the Holy Sacrament, in confessions, Communions, acts of humility, of hope, and love of Jesus Christ! And though the devil should endeavor to terrify her by the faults committed in her younger days, her Spouse, for whom she has left the world, will console her, and thus, full of confidence, she will die in the embraces of her crucified Redeemer, who will conduct her to heaven, that there she may enjoy eternal happiness.

Thus, my dear sister, since you must make choice of a state

of life, make the choice now which you shall wish at death to have made. At death, everyone who sees that for her the world is about to end says, Oh that I had led the life of a saint! Oh that I had left the world and given myself to God! But what is then done, is done, and nothing remains for her but to breathe forth her soul, and to go to hear from Jesus Christ the words, Come, blessed soul, and rejoice with me for eternity; or, Begone forever to hell at a distance from me. You, then, must choose the world or Jesus Christ. If you choose the world, you will probably sooner or later repent of the choice; hence, you ought to reflect well upon it. In the world the number of persons who are lost is very great; in religion, the number of those who are damned is very small. Recommend yourself to Jesus crucified, and to most holy Mary, that they may make you choose the state which is most conducive to your eternal salvation. If you wish to become a nun, resolve to become a saint; if you intend to lead a loose and imperfect life, like some religious, it is useless for you to enter a convent; you should then only lead an unhappy life and die an unhappy death. But if you resolve not to become a religious, I cannot advise you to enter the married state, for St. Paul does not counsel that state to any one, except in case of necessity, which I hope does not exist for you. At least remain in your own house and endeavor to become a saint. I entreat you to say the following prayer for nine days:

My Lord Jesus Christ, who hast died for my salvation, I implore Thee, through the merits of Thy passion, to give me light and strength to choose that state which is best for my salvation. And do thou, O my Mother, Mary, obtain this grace for me by thy powerful intercession.

DISCOURSE TO PIOUS MAIDENS

My dear Sisters in Jesus Christ:

I do not intend to explain the privileges and blessings acquired by those maidens who consecrate their virginity to Jesus Christ; I shall only glance at them.

Excellence of Virginity.

First, they become in the eyes of God as beautiful as the angels of heaven. Baronius relates that upon the death of a holy virgin named Georgia, an immense multitude of doves was seen flying around her; and when the body was carried to the church, they ranged themselves along that part of the roof which corresponded to the situation of the corpse, and did not leave until she was buried. Those doves were thought to be angels who accompanied that virginal body.

Moreover, a maiden who leaves the world, and dedicates herself to Jesus Christ, becomes his spouse. In the Gospel, our Redeemer is called Father, or Master, or Shepherd of our souls; but, with regard to those virgins, he calls himself their spouse; they went out to meet the bridegroom.

When a young woman wishes to establish herself in the world, she will examine, if she be prudent, which of all her suitors is the most noble and the richest. Let us then learn from the Spouse in the sacred Canticles, who well knows—let us learn from her what manner of spouse is he whom consecrated virgins aspire to. Tell me, O sacred Spouse, what manner of spouse is he who makes you the most fortunate of women? My beloved is white, she says, and ruddy, chosen among thousands. He is all white, by reason of his purity;

and ruddy, by reason of the love with which he burns. He is, in fine, so noble and so kind as to be the most amiable of spouses.

With reason, then, did the glorious virgin St, Agnes, as we learn from St. Ambrose, when it was proposed to her to marry the son of the Prefect of Rome, reply that she had a much more advantageous match in view. When some ladies were endeavoring to persuade St. Domitilla to marry Count Aurelian, nephew of the Emperor Domitian, saying there was no obstacle, as he was willing that she should remain a Christian, the saint replied, Tell me, if a monarch and a clown both pretended to a maiden, which would she choose? Now I, should I marry Aurelian, would have to leave the King of Heaven; it would be folly—I will not do so. And thus, in order to remain faithful to Jesus Christ, to whom she had already consecrated her virginity, she was willing to be burned alive, a death which her barbarous suitor caused her to suffer.

Those spouses of Jesus Christ who leave the world for his sake, become his beloved; they are called the first fruits of the lamb: The first fruits to God and to the Lamb Why the first fruits? Because, says Cardinal Ugone, as the first fruits are more grateful than any other to man, so virgins are dearer to God than any others. The divine spouse feeds amongst the lilies: Who feeds amongst the lilies. And what is meant by lilies, if not those devout maidens who consecrate their virginity to Jesus Christ? The Venerable Bede writes that the song of the virgins—that is, the glory which they give to God by preserving untouched the lily of their purity—is far more pleasing to him than the song of all the other saints. Wherefore the Holy Ghost says that there is nothing comparable to virginity. And hence, Cardinal Ugone remarks that dispensations are often granted from other vows, but never from the vow of chastity; and the reason is, because no other treasure can compensate for the loss of that. And it is for the same reason that theologians say, the Blessed Mother would have consented to forego the dignity of Mother of God, could it have been had only at the expense of her virginity.

Who on this earth can conceive the glory which God has prepared for his virgin spouses in paradise? Theologians say that virgins have in heaven their own "Aureola," or special crown of glory, which is refused to the other saints who are not virgins.

But let us come at once to the most important point in our discourse.

This young woman will say, Cannot I become holy in the married state? I do not wish to give you the reply in my own words; hear those of St. Paul, and you will see the difference between the married woman and the virgin: And the unmarried woman, and the virgin, thinketh on the things of the Lord, that she may be holy, both in body and in spirit; but she that is married, thinketh on the things of the world, how she may please her husband? And the Apostle adds: And I speak this for your profit, not for a snare, but for that which is decent, and which may give you power to attend upon the Lord without impediment.

In the first place, I say that married persons can be holy in the spirit, but not in the flesh; on the contrary, virgins who have consecrated their virginity to Jesus Christ are holy both in soul and body. Holy both in body and in spirit; and mark those other words, to attend upon the Lord without impediment. Oh, how many obstacles have not married women to

97

encounter in serving the Lord! And the more noble they are, the greater the obstacles. A woman, to become holy, must adopt the necessary means, which are, much mental prayer, constant use of the sacraments, and continual thought of God. But what time has a married woman for thinking upon God? She that is married thinketh on the things of the world, says St. Paul. The married woman has to think of providing her family with food and raiment. She has to think of rearing her children, of pleasing her husband and her husband's relatives; whence, as the Apostle says, her heart is divided between God, her husband, and her children. Her husband must be attended to; the children cry and scream, and are continually asking for a thousand things. What time can she have to attend to mental prayer, who can scarce attend to all the business of the house? How can she pray amid so many distracting thoughts and disturbances? Scarcely can she go to church, to recollect herself, and communicate upon the Sunday. She may have the good desire, but it will be difficult for her to attend to the things of God as she ought. It is true that in this want of opportunities she may gain merit, by resignation to the will of God, who requires of her, in that state, chiefly patience and resignation; but in the midst of so many distractions and annoyances, without prayer, without meditation, without frequenting the sacraments, it will be morally impossible for her to have that holy patience and resignation.

But would to God that married women had no other evil to contend with besides that of not always being able to attend to their sanctification as much as they should! The greater evil is the danger to which they are continually exposed of losing the grace of God, by reason of the intercourse which they must continually have with the relatives and friends of their husband, as well in their own houses as in the houses of others. Unmarried women do not understand this, but married women and those who have to hear their confessions know it well. Let us, however, now have done with the unhappy life which is led by married women, the ill–treatment that they receive from their husbands, the disobedience of children, the wants of a family, the annoyance of mothers–in–law and relatives, the throes of childbirth, always accompanied by danger of death, not to mention the afflictions of jealousy, and scruples of conscience with regard to the rearing-up of their children,–all of this breeds a tempest under which poor married women have continually to groan; and God grant that in this tempest they may not lose themselves, so as to meet with hell in the other world, after having suffered a hell in this! Such is the unenviable lot of those maidens who choose the world!

But what, such a maiden replies, are there no married women holy? Yes, I answer, there are; but who are they? Such only as become holy through their sufferings, by suffering all from God without finding fault, and with continual patience. And how many married women are to be found in such a state of perfection? They are very rare; and if you find any, they are always in sorrow, that when they could have done so they did not consecrate themselves to Jesus Christ. Amongst all the devout married women I have known, I never knew one to be satisfied with her condition.

The greatest happiness, then, falls to the lot of those maidens who consecrate themselves to Jesus Christ. Those have to encounter none of the dangers which married women must necessarily be placed in. They are not bound to earth by love of children, or men, or dress, or gallantry, whilst married women are obliged to dress with pomp and ornaments, in order to appear with their equals and please their husbands. A maiden who has given herself to Jesus Christ requires only what dress will cover her; nay, she should give scandal if she were to wear any other, or make use of any ornaments. Moreover, virgins have no anxiety about house or children or relatives; their whole care is centred in pleasing Jesus Christ, to whom they have consecrated their soul, their body, and all their love; whence it is that they have more time, and a mind more disengaged for frequent prayer and Communion.

But let us now come to the excuses sometimes brought forward by those who are cold in the love of Jesus Christ.

Such a one will say, I should leave the world if I had some convent to go to, or, at least, if I could always spend my time in devotion at the church when I should please; but I could not remain at home, where I have bad brothers who ill–treat me; and, on the other hand, my parents are unwilling to have me frequent the church. But, I ask you, is it in order to save yourself, or lead an easy life you leave the world? Is it to do your own will or the will of Jesus Christ? If you wish to become holy and serve Jesus Christ, I ask you another question: in what does holiness consist? Holiness does not consist in living in a convent, or spending the entire day in a church, but in being at confession and Communion as often as you can, in obedience, in doing everything assigned you at home, in being retired, in bearing labor and contempt. And if you were to be in a convent, how should you be employed? Do you imagine you should always be either in church or in your cell, or in the refectory, or at recreation? In the convent, although the Sisters have a time marked out for prayer, for Mass, and for Communion, they have also their hours appointed for the business of the house, and more especially the lay–sisters, who, as they do not attend in the choir, have nearly all the labor of the house, and consequently least time for prayer. All exclaim, Let us be in a convent, let us have a convent. How much more easy is it for devout girls to become holy in their own houses than in a convent! How many such have I known to regret having entered a convent, especially when the Community was large, the poor lay–sister in certain offices having scarcely time to say the rosary!

But, Father, such a girl will answer, I have at home a peevish father and mother; I have bad brothers; all of them use me ill; I cannot stand this. Well I say, and if you marry, will you not have to deal with mothers and sisters–in–law, and perhaps undutiful children, and perhaps a harsh husband? Oh, how many cruel husbands are there not, who when first married promised great things, but shortly afterwards ceased to be husbands, and became the tyrants of their wives, treating them not as companions but as slaves? Inquire of many married women whether this be not the fact. But, without going beyond your own home, you all know how your mothers fared. One thing, at least, is certain, that all you should have to surfer at home, after having given yourself to God, you should suffer for the love of Jesus Christ, and he knows how to make your cross sweet and light to you. But how dreadful is it not to suffer for the world's sake!–to suffer without merit! Courage, then, if Jesus Christ has called you to his love, and wishes to have you for his spouse, go on joyfully; it will be his care to afford you consolation even in the midst of sufferings. This, of course, will be only in case you truly love him, and live as his spouse.

Means to preserve Virginal Purity.

Hear, then, for the last time, the means that you are to adopt in order to become holy, and live a true spouse of Jesus

101

Christ; and these are, to practise the virtues becoming his spouse. We read in the Gospel 1 that the kingdom of heaven is likened unto virgins. But to what virgins? Not to the foolish, but to the wise. The wise were admitted to the nuptials, but the door was shut in the face of the foolish; to whom the spouse said, I know you not—you are indeed virgins, but I do not acknowledge you for my spouses. The true spouses of Jesus Christ follow the spouse whithersoever he goeth. These follow the Lamb whithersoever he goeth. What is the meaning of following the Lamb? St. Augustine says that it means the imitation of the Lamb both in body and mind. After you have consecrated your body to him, you must consecrate to him your whole heart, so that your heart may be entirely devoted to his love; and, therefore, you must adopt all the means that are necessary for making you belong entirely to Jesus Christ.

1. The first of those means is mental prayer, to which you must be most attentive. But do not imagine that, in order to pray thus, it is necessary for you to be in a convent, or remain all day in the church. It is true that at home there is much disturbance created by the persons there; nevertheless, those who wish can find time and place for prayer: this is in the morning before the others rise, and at night after the others have gone to bed. In order to pray, it is not necessary to be always on bended knees; you can pray whilst laboring, and even when walking out on business (should, you have no other opportunity), by raising your soul to God, and thinking on the Passion of Jesus Christ, or any other pious subject.

2. The second means is, the frequentation of the sacraments of confession and Communion. With regard to confession, each one has to make choice of a confessor, whom she is to

obey in everything, otherwise she will never walk steadily in the way of perfection. As to Communion, she must not depend solely upon obedience; she must desire it, and ask for it. This divine food must be hungered after; Jesus Christ must be desired. It is frequent Communion that renders his spouses faithful to Jesus Christ, especially in the preservation of holy purity. The Most Holy Sacrament preserves the soul in every virtue; and it appears that its most special effect is to preserve untouched the chastity of virgins, according to that of the prophet, who calls this sacrament the corn of the elect, and wine springing forth virgins.

3. The third means is, retirement and caution: As the lily amongst the thorns, so is my beloved amongst the daughters. For a virgin to think of remaining faithful to Jesus Christ amid the conversations, the jests, and other amusements of the world, is useless; it is necessary that she preserve herself amid the thorns of abstinence and mortification, by using not only the greatest modesty and reserve in speaking with men, but even all austerity and penitential exercises when necessary. Such are the thorns which preserve the lilies; I mean young maidens, who otherwise should soon be lost. The Lord calls the cheeks of his spouse as beautiful as those of the turtle: Thy cheeks are beautiful as the turtle dove's. And why so? Because the turtle, by instinct, avoids the company of other birds, and always remains alone. That virgin, then, appears beautiful in the eyes of Jesus Christ who does all that she can to hide herself from the eyes of others. St. Jerome says that Jesus is a jealous spouse. Hence he is much displeased when he sees a virgin dedicated to him endeavoring to appear before men to please them. Pious maidens endeavor to appear repulsive, that they may not attract men. The Venerable Sister Catharine of Jesus, afterwards a Teresian nun, washed her face with the filthy water of tar, and

then designedly exposed her face to the sun, that she might lose her complexion. St. Andregesina having, as we are told by Bollandus, been promised in marriage, prayed the Lord to deform her, and was heard, for she was immediately covered with a leprosy which caused everyone to avoid her; and as soon as her suitor had ceased his offers, her former beauty was restored. It is related by James di Viatrico that there was a certain virgin in a convent whose eyes had inflamed a prince. The latter threatened to set fire to the monastery if she would not yield to him; but she plucked out her eyes and sent them to him in a basin, the bearer of which was instructed to say, "Here are the darts which have wounded your heart–take them, and leave me my soul untouched." The same author tells of St. Euphemia, that, having been promised by her father to a certain count, who left no means untried to obtain her, she, in order to free herself from his addresses, cut off her nose and lips, saying to herself, "Vain beauty, you shall never be to me an occasion of sin!" St. Antoninus tells something similar (and his account is confirmed by Baronius) of the Abbess Ebba, who, fearing an invasion of the barbarians, cut off her nose and upper lip to the teeth; and that all the other nuns, to the number of thirty, following her example, did the same. The barbarians came, and seeing them so deformed, set fire to the monastery through rage and burned them alive; and hence the Church, as Baronius tells us, has enrolled them among her martyrs. This is not allowable for others to do; those saints did so by the especial impulse of the Holy Ghost. But it sufficiently well answers the purpose of showing you what virgins who loved Jesus Christ have done to prevent men from seeking them. Devout virgins at present should at least move as modestly, and be seen as little as possible by men. Should it happen that a virgin should, by chance, and without any fault of hers, receive by violence any insult from men, be it known to you that after it she will remain as pure as before. St. Lucia made an answer of this kind to the tyrant who threatened to dishonor her. "If you do," she said, "And I be so treated against my will, my crown shall be double." It is the consent only that is hurtful; and know, moreover, that if a virgin be modest and reserved, men will have no inclination to interfere with her.

4. The fourth means of preserving purity is the mortification of the senses. St. Basil says, "A virgin should not be immodest in any respect,–in tongue, ears, eyes, touch, and still less in mind." A virgin, in order to keep herself pure, must be modest in her speech, conversing seldom with men, and that only through necessity, and in few words. Her ears must be pure, by not listening to worldly conversations. Her eyes must be pure, by being either closed, or fixed upon the earth in the presence of men. She must be pure in touch, using therein all possible caution, both as regards herself and others. She must be pure in spirit, by resisting all immodest thoughts, through the help of Jesus and Mary. And to this end, she must mortify herself with fasting, abstinence, and other penitential exercises; which things she must not practise without the consent of her confessor, otherwise they should injure her soul by making her proud. Those acts of penance must not be made without the confessor's permission, but they must be de sired and sought for; for the confessor, if he does not see the penitent wishing for them, will not give them. Jesus is a spouse of blood, who espoused our souls upon the cross, whereon he shed all his blood for us. A bloody spouse art thou to me. Therefore those spouses who love him, love tribulation, infirmity, sorrows, ill–treatment, and injuries; and receive them not only with patience, but with joy. Thus may we understand that passage which says that virgins follow the Lamb whithersoever He goeth. They follow their spouse Jesus with joy and gladness whith-

ersoever he goeth, even through sorrow and disgrace, as has been done by so many holy virgins, who have followed him to torments and to death, smiling and rejoicing.

5. Finally, Sisters, in order that you may obtain perseverance in this holy life, you must recommend yourselves often and much to Most Holy Mary, the Queen of Virgins. She is the mediatrix who negotiates those espousals, and brings virgins to espouse her Son. After her shall virgins be brought to the King. It is she, in fine, who obtains fidelity for those chosen spouses; for, without her assistance, they should be all unfaithful.

CONCLUSION.

Come on, then, you who intend to live no longer for the world, but for Jesus Christ alone. (I address myself to those who feel themselves called by that divine Spouse to consecrate themselves to his love.) I do not wish that you should make any vow this morning, or oblige yourselves at once to perpetual chastity. You should do that when God inspires you, and your confessor is willing. I only desire you by a simple act, and without any obligation, to thank Jesus Christ for having called you to his love; and to offer yourselves to him henceforward for your entire lives. Say then to him:

O my Jesus, my God, and my Redeemer, who hast died for me, compassionate me who burn to call myself Thy spouse. I burn, because I see that Thou hast called me to that honor; nor do I know how to thank Thee for that grace. I should now have been in hell; and Thou, instead of chastising me, hast called me to be Thy spouse. Yes, my spouse, I leave the world, I leave all through love of Thee, and give myself entirely to Thee. What world?—what world do I speak of? My

Jesus, henceforward Thou art to be my only good—my only love. I see that Thou wishest to have my entire heart, and I wish to resign it entirely to Thee. Receive me in Thy mercy, and do not reject me as I have deserved that Thou shouldst. Forget all the offences that I have given Thee, of which I repent with my whole soul; would that I had died before offending Thee! Pardon me; inflame me with Thy holy love, and give me Thy aid, in order that I may be faithful to Thee, and never leave Thee more. Thou, my spouse, hast given Thyself all to me. Behold! I give myself entirely to Thee. Mary, my Queen and my Mother, chain my heart to that of Jesus Christ; and fasten both hearts so that they be never sundered more.

I leave you now my blessing, in order that you may be so bound to Jesus Christ as never again to depart from him. Give your hearts now to Jesus Christ; say, Jesus, my spouse, henceforward I wish to love only Thee, and nothing else.

THE VOCATION TO THE PRIESTHOOD

I.

Necessity of a Divine Vocation to take Holy Orders.

To enter any state of life, a divine vocation is necessary; for without such a vocation it is, if not impossible, at least most difficult to fulfil the obligations of our state, and obtain salvation. But if for all states a vocation is necessary, it is necessary in a particular manner for the ecclesiastical state. He that entereth not by the door into the sheepfold, but climbeth up another way, the same is a thief and a robber. Hence he who takes holy orders without a call from God is convicted of theft, in taking by force a dignity which God does not wish to bestow upon him. And before him St. Paul said the same thing: Neither doth any man take the honor to himself, but he that is called by God, as Aaron was. So Christ also did not glorify Himself that He might be made a high priest; but he that said unto Him: Thou art My Son, this day I have begotten Thee.

No one, then, however learned, prudent, and holy he may be, can thrust himself into the sanctuary unless he is first called and introduced by God. Jesus Christ himself, who among all men was certainly the most learned and the most holy, full of grace and truth, in whom are hid all the treasures of wisdom and knowledge,—Jesus Christ, I say, required a divine call in order to assume the dignity of the priesthood.

In entering the sanctuary, even after God himself had called them to it, the saints trembled. When his bishop ordered St. Augustine to receive ordination, the saint through humility regarded the command as a chastisement of his sins. To escape the priesthood St. Ephrem of Syria feigned madness; and St. Ambrose pretended to be a man of a cruel disposition.

To avoid the priesthood, St. Ammonius the Monk cut off his ears, and threatened to pluck out his tongue, if the persons who pressed him to take holy orders should continue to molest him. In a word, St. Cyril of Alexandria says, "The saints have dreaded the dignity of the priesthood as a burden of enormous weight." Can anyone, then, says St. Cyprian, be so daring as to attempt of himself, and without a divine call, to assume the priesthood?

As a vassal who would of himself take the office of minister should violate the authority of his sovereign, so he who intrudes himself into the sanctuary without a vocation violates the authority of God. How great should be the temerity of the subject who, without the appointment, and even in opposition to the will of the monarch, should attempt to administer the royal patrimony, to decide lawsuits, to command the army, and to assume the viceregal authority? "Among you," asks St. Bernard in speaking to clerics, "is there any one so insolent as, without orders and contrary to the will of the pettiest monarch, to assume the direction of his affairs?" And are not priests, as St. Prosper says, the administrators of the royal house? Are they not, according to St. Ambrose, the "leaders and rectors of the flock of Christ?" according to St. Chrysostom, the "interpreters of the divine judgments," and according to St. Denis, the "Vicars of Christ?" Will anyone who knows all this dare to become the minister of God without a divine call?

To think of exercising royal authority is, according to St. Peter Chrysologus, criminal in a subject. To intrude into the house of a private individual, in order to dispose of his goods and to manage his business, would be considered temerity; for even a private individual has the right of appointing the administrators of his affairs. And will you, says St. Bernard, without being called or introduced by God, intrude into his house to take charge of his interests and to dispose of his goods?

The Council of Trent has declared that the Church regards not as her minister, but as a robber, the man who audaciously assumes the priesthood without a vocation. Such priests may labor and toil, but their labors shall profit them little before God. On the contrary, the works which are meritorious in others shall deserve chastisement for them. Should a servant who is commanded by his master to take care of the house, through his own caprice labor in cultivating the vineyard, he may toil and sweat, but instead of being rewarded he shall be chastised by his master. Thus, in the first place, because they are not conformable to the divine will, the Lord shall not accept the toils of the man who, without a vocation, intrudes himself into the priesthood. I have no pleasure in you, saith the Lord, of Hosts, and I will not receive a gift of your hand. In the end God will not reward, but will punish the works of the priest who has entered the sanctuary without a vocation. What stranger so ever cometh to it (the tabernacle), shall be slain.

Whosoever, then, aspires to holy orders must, in the first place, carefully examine if his vocation is from God. "For," says St. John Chrysostom, "the more sublime the dignity, the more should one assure one's self of a divine vocation." Now to know whether his call is from God, he should examine the marks of a divine vocation. He, says St. Luke, who wishes to build a tower, first computes the necessary expenses, in order to know if he has the means of completing the edifice.

II.

Marks of a Divine Vocation to the Sacerdotal State.

Let us now see what are the marks of a divine vocation to the sacerdotal state.

Nobility is not a mark of a divine vocation. To know, says St. Jerome, whether a person should become the guide of the people in what regards their eternal salvation, we must consider not nobility of blood, but sanctity of life. "When God wishes to raise any one to a dignity, he regulates his choice according to the sanctity of life, and not according to the titles of nobility."

Nor is the will of parents a mark of a divine vocation. In inducing a child to take priesthood, they seek not his spiritual welfare, but their own interest, and the advancement of the family. "How many mothers," says St. John Chrysostom, or the author of The Imperfect Work, have eyes only for the bodies of their children and disdain their souls! To see them happy here below is all that they desire; as for the punishments that perhaps their children are to endure in the next life, they do not even think of them. Oh, how many priests shall we see condemned on the day of judgment for having taken holy orders to please their relatives!

Neither nobility of birth, nor the will of parents, is a mark of a vocation to the priesthood; nor is talent or fitness for the offices of a priest a sign of vocation; for along with talent, a holy life and a divine call are necessary. What, then, are the marks of a divine vocation to the ecclesiastical state?

1. PURITY OF INTENTION.

The first is a good intention. It is necessary to enter the sanctuary by the door; but there is no other door than Jesus Christ: I am the door of the sheep. . . . By me, if any man enter in, he shall be saved. To enter, then, by the door, is to become a priest not to please relatives, nor to advance the family, nor for the sake of self–interest or self–esteem, but to serve God, to propagate his glory, and to save souls. "If anyone," says a wise theologian, the learned continuator of Tournely, "Presents himself for Holy Orders without any vicious affection and with the sole desire to be employed in the service of God and in the salvation of his neighbor, he, we may believe, is called by God." Another author asserts that he who is impelled by ambition, interest, or a motive of his own glory, is called not by God, but by the devil. "But," adds St. Anselm, "he who enters the priesthood through so unworthy motives shall receive not a blessing, but a male-diction, from God."

2. SCIENCE AND TALENTS.

The second mark is the talent and learning necessary for the fulfilment of the duties of a priest. Priests must be masters to teach the people the law of God. For the lips of the priest shall keep knowledge, and they shall seek the law at his mouth. Sidonius Apollinarius used to say, "Ignorant physicians are the cause of many deaths." An ignorant priest, particularly a confessor, who teaches false doctrines and gives bad counsels, will be the ruin of many souls; because, in consequence of being a priest, his errors are easily believed.

Hence, Ivone Carnotensis has written: "No one should be admitted to Holy Orders unless he has given sufficient proofs of good conduct and learning."

A priest must not only have a competent knowledge of all the rubrics necessary for the celebration of Mass, but must be also acquainted with the principal things which regard the sacrament of penance. It is true, every priest is not obliged to hear confessions, unless there is great necessity for his assistance in the district in which he lives; however, every priest is bound to be acquainted with what a priest must ordinarily know in order to be able to hear the confessions of dying persons; that is, he is bound to know when he has faculties to absolve, when and how he ought to give absolution to the sick, whether conditionally or absolutely; what obligation he ought to impose on them if they are under any censure. He should also know at least the general principles of moral theology.

3. POSITIVE GOODNESS OF CHARACTER.

The third mark of an ecclesiastical vocation is positive virtue.

Hence, in the first place, the person who is to be ordained should be a man of innocent life, and should not be contaminated by sins. The Apostle requires that they who are to be ordained priests should be free from every crime. In ancient times, a person who had committed a single mortal sin could never be ordained, as we learn from the First Council of Nice. And St. Jerome says that it was not enough for a person to be free from sin at the time of his ordination, but that it was, moreover, necessary that he should not have fallen into mortal sin since the time of his baptism. It is true

113

that this rigorous discipline has ceased in the Church, but it has been always at least required that he who had fallen into grievous sins should purify his conscience for a considerable time before his ordination. This we may infer from a letter to the Archbishop of Rheims, in which Alexander III. commanded that a deacon who had wounded another deacon, if he sincerely repented of his sin, might, after being absolved, and after performing the penance enjoined, be permitted again to exercise his order; and that if he afterwards led a perfect life, he might be promoted to priesthood. He, then, who finds himself bound by a habit of any vice cannot take any Holy Order without incurring the guilt of mortal sin. "I am horrified," says St. Bernard, "When I think whence thou comest, whither thou goest, and what a short penance thou hast put between thy sins and thy ordination. However, it is indispensable that thou do not undertake to purify the conscience of others before thou purifiest thy own." Of those daring sinners who, though full of bad habits, take priesthood, an ancient author, Gildas, says, "It is not to the priesthood that they should be admitted, but to the pillory." They, then, says St. Isidore, who are still subject to the habit of any sin should not be promoted to Holy Orders.

But he who intends to ascend the altar must not only be free from sin, but must have also begun to walk in the path of perfection, and have acquired a habit of virtue. In our Moral Theology, we have shown in a distinct dissertation (and this is the common opinion) that if a person in the habit of any vice wish to be ordained, it is not enough for him to have the dispositions necessary for the sacrament of penance, but that he must also have the dispositions required for receiving the sacrament of Holy Orders; otherwise he is unfit for both: and should he receive absolution with the intention of taking Orders without the necessary dispositions, he, and the confessor who absolves him, will be guilty of a grievous sin. For it is not enough for those who wish to take Holy Orders to have got out of the state of sin; they must also, according to the words of Alexander III.–cited in the preceding paragraph–have the true positive virtue necessary for the ecclesiastical state. From the words of the pontiff we learn that a person who has done penance may exercise an order already received, but he who has only done penance cannot take a higher order. The Angelic Doctor teaches the same doctrine: "Sanctity is required for the reception of Holy Orders, and we must place the sublime burden of the priesthood only upon walls already dried by sanctity; that is, freed from the malignant humor of sin." This is conformable to what St. Denis wrote long before: "Let no one be so bold as to propose himself to others as their guide in the things of God, if he has not first, with all his power, transformed himself into God to the point of perfect resemblance to him." For this St. Thomas adduces two reasons: the first is, that as he who takes orders is raised above seculars in dignity, so he should be superior to them in sanctity. The second reason is, that by his ordination a priest is appointed to exercise the most sublime ministry on the altar, for which greater sanctity is required than for the religious state.

Hence the Apostle forbade Timothy to ordain neophytes; that is, according to St. Thomas, neophytes in perfection as well as neophytes in age. Hence the Council of Trent, in reference to the words of Scripture, And a spotless life in old age, prescribes to the bishops to admit to ordination only those who show themselves worthy by a conduct full of wise maturity. And of this positive virtue, it is necessary, according to St. Thomas, to have not a doubtful but a certain knowledge. This, according to St. Gregory, is particularly necessary with regard to the virtue of chastity. With regard to chastity the

Holy Pontiff required a proof of many years.

III.

To what Dangers one exposes one's self by entering Holy Orders without a Vocation.

From what has been said, it follows that he who takes Holy Orders without the marks of a vocation cannot be excused from the guilt of grievous sin. This is the doctrine of many theologians, – of Habert, of Natalis Alexander, and of the continuator of Tournely. And before them St. Augustine taught the same. Speaking of the chastisement inflicted on Core, Dathan, and Abiron, who, without being called, attempted to exercise the sacerdotal functions, the holy Doctor said: "God struck them that they might serve as an example, and thus to warn off him who would dare to assume a sacred charge. Indeed, this is the chastisement reserved for those who would thrust themselves into the office of bishop, priest, or deacon." And the reason is, first, because he who thrusts himself into the sanctuary without a divine call cannot be excused from grievous presumption; secondly, because he will be deprived of the congruous and abundant helps without which, as Habert writes, he will be absolutely unable to comply with the obligations of his state, but will fulfil them only with very great difficulty. He will be like a dislocated member, which can be used only with difficulty, and which causes deformity.

Hence Bishop Abelly writes: "He who of himself, without inquiring whether he has a vocation or not, thrusts himself into the priesthood will no doubt expose himself to the great danger of losing his soul; for he commits against the Holy Spirit that sin for which, as the Gospel says, there is hardly or very rarely any pardon."

The Lord has declared that his wrath is provoked against those who wish to rule in his Church without being called by him. On this passage St. Gregory says, "It is by themselves and not by the will of the Supreme Head that they reign." Divine vocation is entirely wanting to them, and they have followed only the ardor of vile cupidity, not certainly to accept, but to usurp this sublime dignity. How many intrigues, adulations, entreaties, and other means, do certain persons employ in order to procure ordination, not in obedience to the call of God, but through earthly motives? But woe to such men, says the Lord by the prophet Isaias: Woe to you, apostate children, . . . that you would take counsel, and not of me. On the day of judgment they shall claim a reward, but Jesus Christ shall cast them off. Many will say to Me in that day, have we not prophesied in Thy name (by preaching and teaching), and cast out devils in Thy name (by absolving penitent sinners), and done many miracles in Thy name (by correcting the wicked, by settling disputes, by converting sinners). And then will I profess unto them: I never knew you; depart from me, you that work iniquity. Priests who have not been called are indeed workmen and ministers of God, because they have received the sacerdotal character; but they are ministers of iniquity and rapine, because they have of their own will, and without vocation, intruded themselves into the sheepfold. They have not, as St. Bernard says, received the keys, but have taken them by force. They toil, but God will not accept; he will, on the contrary, punish their works and labors, because they have not entered the sanctuary by the straight path. The labor of fools shall afflict them that know not how to go to the city. The Church, says St. Leo, receives only those whom the Lord chooses, and by his election makes fit to be his ministers. But, on the other hand, the Church rejects those whom, as St. Peter Damian has written, God has not called; for instead of promoting her

117

welfare, they commit havoc among her members; and instead of edifying, they contaminate and destroy her children.

Whom He (the Lord) shall choose, they shall approach to Him. God will gladly admit into his presence all whom he has called to the priesthood, and will cast off the priest whom he has not chosen. St. Ephrem regards as lost the man who is so daring as to take the order of priesthood without a vocation. And Peter de Blois has written: "What ruin does not prepare for himself the bold man who of the sacrifice makes a sacrilege, and of life an instrument of death." He who errs in his vocation exposes himself to greater danger than if he transgressed particular precepts; for if he violates a particular command, he may rise from his fault, and begin again to walk in the right path; but he who errs in his vocation mistakes the way itself. Hence the longer he travels in it, the more distant he is from his home. To him we may justly apply the words of St. Augustine: "You run well, but the wrong road."

It is necessary to be persuaded of the truth of what St. Gregory says, that our eternal salvation depends principally on embracing the state to which God has called us. The reason is evident; for it is God that destines, according to the order of his providence, his state of life for each individual, and, according to the state to which he calls him, prepares for him abundant graces and suitable helps. "In the distribution of his graces," says St. Cyprian, "the Holy Spirit takes into consideration his own plan and not our caprices." And according to the Apostle: And whom He predestinated; them He also called. And whom He called, them He also justified. Thus to vocation succeeds justification, and to justification, glory; that is, the attainment of eternal life. He, then, who does not obey the call of God, shall neither be justified nor glorified. Father Granada justly said that vocation is the main wheel of our entire life. As in a clock, if the main wheel be spoiled, the entire clock is injured, so, says St. Gregory Nazianzen, if a person err in his vocation, his whole life will be full of errors; for in the state to which God has not called him, he will be deprived of the helps by which he can with facility lead a good life.

Everyone, says St. Paul, hath his proper gift from God; one after this manner, and another after that. The meaning of this passage, according to St. Thomas and other commentators, is, that the Lord gives to each one graces to fulfil with ease the obligations of the state to which he calls him. "God," says the Angelic Doctor, "gives to every man not only certain aptitudes, but also all that is necessary to exercise them." And in another place he writes: "God does not destine men to such or such a vocation without favoring them with gifts at the same time, and preparing them in such a way as to render them capable of fulfilling the duties of their vocation; for says St. Paul: Our sufficiency is from God, who also hath made us fit ministers of the New Testament. As each person, then, will be able to discharge with facility the office to which God elects him, so he will be unfit for the fulfilment of the office to which God does not call him. The foot which is given to enable us to walk cannot see; the eye, which is given to see is incapable of hearing; and how shall he who is not chosen by God to the priesthood be able to discharge its obligations?

It belongs to the Lord to choose the workmen who are to cultivate his vineyard: I have chosen you . . . and have appointed you that you should go, and should bring forth fruit. Hence the Redeemer did not say, Beg of men to go and gather the harvest; but he tells us to ask the master of the crop to send workmen to collect it. Hence he also said, As the Father hath sent Me, I also send you. When God calls, he himself, says St. Leo, gives the necessary helps. This is what Jesus Christ has said: I am the door. By Me if any man enter in he shall be saved, and he shall go in, and go out, and shall find pasture. "He shall go in:" what the priest called by God undertakes, he shall easily accomplish without sin, and with merit. And shall go out . 1 he shall be in the midst of perils and occasions of sin, but with the divine aid he shall readily escape injury. And shall find pastures: finally, in consequence of being in the state in which God has placed him, he will be assisted in all the duties of his ministry by special graces, which will make him advance in perfection. Hence he will be able to say with confidence, The Lord ruleth me: and I shall want nothing. He hath set me in a place of pasture.

But priests whom God has not sent to work in his Church, he shall abandon to eternal ignominy and destruction. I did not send prophets, says the Lord by the prophet Jeremiah, yet they ran. He afterwards adds: Therefore I will take you away, carrying you, and will for sake you . . . and I will bring an everlasting reproach upon you, and a perpetual shame which shall never be forgotten.

In order to be raised to the sublimity of the priesthood, it is necessary, as St. Thomas says, for a man "To be exalted and elevated by divine power above the natural order of things," because he is appointed the sanctifier of the people, and the vicar of Jesus Christ. But in him who raises himself to so great a dignity shall be verified the words of the Wise Man: There is that hath appeared a fool after he was lifted up on high. Had he remained in the world, he should perhaps have been a virtuous layman; but having become a priest without a vocation, he will be a bad priest, and instead of promoting the interest of religion, he will do great injury to the Church. Of such priests the Roman Catechism says: "Such ministers are for the Church of God the gravest embarrassment and the most terrible scourge." And what good can be expected from the priest who has entered the sanctuary without a vocation? "It is impossible." says St. Leo, "That a work so badly begun should finish well." St. Laurence Justinian has written: "What fruit, I ask, can come from a corrupted root?" Our Saviour has said, Every plant which my heavenly Father hath not planted, shall be rooted up. Hence Peter de Blois writes that when God permits a person to be ordained without a vocation, the permission is not a grace but a chastisement. For a tree which has not taken deep root, when exposed to the tempest, shall soon fall and be cast into the fire. And St. Bernard says that he who has not lawfully entered the sanctuary shall continue to be unfaithful; and instead of procuring the salvation of souls, he shall be the cause of their death and perdition. This is conformable to the doctrine of Jesus Christ: He that entereth not by the door into the sheepfold, . . . the same is a thief and a robber.

Some may say, if they only were admitted to orders who have the marks of vocation which have been laid down as indispensable, there should be but few priests in the Church, and the people should be left without the necessary helps. But to this the Fourth Council of
Lateran has answered: "It is much better to confer the priesthood on a small number of virtuous clerics than to have a large number of bad priests." And St. Thomas says that God never abandons his Church so as to leave her in want of fit ministers to provide for the necessity of the people. St. Leo justly says that to provide for the wants of the people by bad priests would be not to save but to destroy them.

APPENDIX.

MEANS TO BE ADOPTED IN ORDER
TO KNOW ONE'S VOCATION.

We collect and briefly indicate in this Appendix the principal means by which one may easily arrive at the knowledge of God's designs relatively to the state of life that one should embrace.

I.

It is, above all, of the highest importance that the heart be free from sin; the Lord loves to communicate himself to those who have a pure heart: Blessed are the clean of heart; for they shall see God.

II.

Let your conduct be well regulated. For this purpose, see the Rule of Life which St. Alphonsus offers you, and try to follow it faithfully.

III.

Look upon the affair of choosing a state of life, in accordance with the will of God, as a matter of your greatest concern, since on the choice that you make depends your eternal salvation.

IV.

Have a good intention and a sincere desire to know and to do the will of God, whatever it may be. It is, therefore, necessary that you hold yourself entirely detached and in a pious indifference in regard to all the states of life, in order not to put any obstacle in the way of the movements of grace, as you have seen above.

V.

Carefully avoid dissipation; at least, retire into the solitude of your heart, after the example of St. Catharine of Sienna, always remembering that God is near you, and that he wishes to speak to your heart. You will understand his voice the more quickly and the more distinctly, the less you communicate with the world.

VI.

St. Alphonsus explains to you at length, in the letter quoted above, the utility of a retreat. If it is not in your power to make it, either at home or in some religious house, where you may find all that you require for this purpose, try to supply its place by leading a retired life, and by frequently meditating on the Last Things. Nothing is more apt to enlighten you and to keep you in a good disposition.

VII.

In your doubts consult a wise director, who, as the representative of God, may instruct you and guide you in a safe manner.

VIII.

Let the grace of knowing your vocation and of faithfully corresponding to it be the only, or at least the principal, object that you have in view in all your exercises of piety,– in your meditations, Communions, prayer, mortifications, and all your good works.

IX.

Ordinarily, the Lord does not delay to enlighten those who have recourse to him, especially in behalf of a cause so holy and so agreeable to his heart. If, however, he would leave you in uncertainty for a time more or less long, to try your fidelity, to purify you more, or to strengthen you and raise you to a very high perfection, take care not to relax in anything; humbly resign yourself, and wait with confidence and in peace for the break of day; for your Heavenly Father will surely hear you and your perseverance will not fail to be crowned with success.

X.

While waiting for the Lord to enlighten you, do not be less faithful in fulfilling all your duties in the condition of life in which his divine Providence has placed you. It would be a great fault to neglect your actual duties in the expectation of a change; God would withdraw his hand, instead of stretching it forth to aid you.

XI.

In general, the following are the principal signs of a true vocation:

1. A GOOD INTENTION; that is, the intention to embrace such a state only to please God and to arrive more surely at the haven of salvation.

2. THE INCLINATION and THE APTITUDE to exercise the duties proper to this state.

3. THE KNOWLEDGE of the duties that this state imposes, and the FIRM WILL to fulfil them till the end.

4. THAT THERE is NO GRAVE IMPEDIMENT, such as the great poverty in which one might leave one's father or one's mother.

5. THE FAVORABLE ADVICE of a wise director.

HYMN

Sighs of Love to Jesus Christ.

THE SOUL THAT GIVES ITSELF ALL TO JESUS.

World, thou art no more for me;
World, I am no more for thee; −
All affections, dear or sweet,
All are laid at Jesus' feet.

He has so enamoured me
Of his heavenly charity,
That no earthly goods inspire
Aught of love or vain desire.

Jesus, Love, be Thou my own;
Thee I long for, − Thee alone;
All myself I give to Thee,
Do whate'er Thou wilt with me.

Life without Thy love would be
Death, O Sovereign Good, to me.
Bound and held by Thy dear chains,
Captive now my heart remains.

O my Life, my soul from Thee
Can henceforth no longer flee;
By Thy loving arrows slain,
Now Thy prey it must remain.

If ungrateful worms like me
Merit not the love of Thee,
Thou, sweet Lord, hast well deserved

To be ever loved and served.

Then, O God, my heart inflame;
Give that love which Thou dost claim;
Payment I will ask for none,
Love demands but love alone.

God of Beauty, Lord of Light!
Thy good will is my delight;
Now henceforth Thy will divine
Ever shall in all be mine.

Come, O Jesus, I implore,
Pierce Thy heart, 'tis mine no more;
Kindle in my breast Thy fire,
That of love I may expire.

Ah, my Spouse, I love but Thee;
Thou my Love shall ever be.
Thee I love; I love and sigh
For Thy love one day to die.

Other Titles Available from
St Athanasius Press
www.stathanasiuspress.com

Be sure to check our web site for the newest titles being offered and for our latest contact information!

A Commonitory for the Antiquity and Universality
of the Catholic Faith Against the
Profane Novelties of all Heresies
by Vincent of Lerins

A Golden Book of Three Tabernacles:
Poverty, Humility and Patience
by Thomas A Kempis

A Little Book of Eternal Wisdom
by Blessed Henry Suso

A Short Catechism of Cardinal Bellarmine
by Cardinal Robert Bellarmine

A Thought from St Ignatius Loyola
for Each Day of the Year
by St Ignatius Loyola

A Thought From Thomas A Kempis
for Each Day of the Year
by Thomas A Kempis

A Treatise of Discretion
by St Catherine of Siena

A Treatise of Divine Providence
& A Treatise of Obedience
by St Catherine of Siena

A Treatise of Prayer
by St Catherine of Siena

A Treatise on the Particular Examen of Conscious
by Fr Luis De La Palma, SJ

Catholic An Essential and Exclusive Attribute
of the True Church
by Rt Rev Msgr Capel

Christ Our Rest and King
by Henry Edward Manning

Cochems Explanation of the Holy Sacrifice of the Mass
by Fr Martin Cochem

Collection of Catholic Prayers and Devotions

Collection of Thomas A Kempis Classics
by Thomas A Kempis

Devotion to the Nine Choirs of Angels
by Henri Marie Boudon

Devotion to the Sacred Heart of Jesus
by Fr John Croiset, SJ

Dignity and Duties of the Priest or Selva
by St Alphonsus M Liguori, CSSR

Explanation of the Psalms & Canticles
in the Divine Office
by St Alphonsus M Liguori, CSSR

For Passion Sunday
by Thomas A Kempis

General Catholic Devotions
Compiled by Rev Bonaventure Hammer, OFM

Humility of Heart
by Fr Cajetan Mary da Bergamo

Indifferentism or
Is One Religion as Good as Another?
by John Maclaughlin

Life of St Leonard of Port Maurice
by Fr Dominic Devas, OFM

Mental Prayer and the Exercises of a Retreat
by St Alphonsus M Liguori, CSSR

Modernism
by Cardinal Mercier

On Cleaving to God English/Latin
by St Albert the Great

On Contempt for the World or
De Contemptu Mundi
by St Eucherius of Lyon

On Divine Love and the Means of Acquiring It
by St Alphonsus M Liguori, CSSR

2 Volume Set
Personal Recollections of Joan of Arc
by Mark Twain

Preparation for Death
by St Alphonsus M Liguori, CSSR

Reasonableness of Catholic Ceremonies and Practices
by Rev John J. Burke

Religious Orders of Women
in the United States (1930 Photos included)
by Elinor Tong Dehey

Saint Athanasius:
The Father of Orthodoxy
by F. A. Forbes

Saint Vincent de Paul
by F. A. Forbes

Sermons for All the Sundays in the Year
by St Alphonsus M Liguori, CSSR

Sermons Upon Various Subjects
by St Alphonsus M Liguori, CSSR

St Alphonsus Liguori on the Council of Trent
by St Alphonsus M Liguori, CSSR

St Charity: A True Life Catholic Pro Life Story
by Mel Waller

Ten Reasons Proposed to His Adversaries
for Disputation in the Name of the Faith
by St Edmund Campion

The Art of Dying Well
by St Robert Bellarmine

The Autobiography of St Ignatius Loyola
by St Ignatius Loyola

The Choice of a State of Life and the
Vocation to the Religious State
by St Alphonsus M Liguori, CSSR

The Cross and the Shamrock
by Hugh Quigley

The Cure of Ars
by Kathleen O'Meara

The Dialogue of the Seraphic Virgin
St Catherine of Siena
by St Catherine of Siena

The Douay Catechism of 1649
by Henry Tuberville, D.D.

The Eternal Happiness of the Saints
by St Robert Bellarmine

The Grace of Prayer is Given to All
by St Alphonsus M Liguori, CSSR

The Great Means of Salvation and of Perfection
by St Alphonsus M Liguori, CSSR

The History of Heresies
by St Alphonsus M Liguori, CSSR

The Holy Eucharist
by St Alphonsus M Liguori, CSSR

The Holy Ways of the Cross
by Henri Marie Boudon

The Life of St Dominic Savio
by St John Bosco

The Life of Saint Columba
by F. A. Forbes

The Life of Saint Monica
by F. A. Forbes

The Little Kempis
or Short Sayings and Prayers
by Thomas A Kempis

The Love of Souls Or
Reflections and Affections
on the Passion of Jesus Christ
by St Alphonsus M Liguori, CSSR

The Maxims and Sayings of St Philip Neri
by St Philip Neri

The Mind's Road to God
by St Bonaventure

3 Volume Set
The Practice of Christian and Religious Perfection
by Fr Alphonsus Rodriguez, SJ

The Practice of the Love of Jesus Christ
by St Alphonsus M Liguori, CSSR

The Practice of the Presence of God
by Brother Lawrence (Nicholas Herman of Lorraine)
Carmelite Lay Brother

The Psalter of the Blessed Virgin Mary
by St Bonaventure

The Raccolta or A Manual of Indulgences
1957 Edition

The Roman Index of Forbidden Books
by Francis S Betten, SJ

The Spiritual Conflict and Conquest
by Dom J Castaniza, OSB

The Treatise on Purgatory
by St Catherine of Genoa

The Triumph of the Cross
by Fra Girolamo Savonarola

The Valley of Lilies & The Little Garden of Roses
by Thomas A Kempis

The Way of Salvation and Perfection
by St Alphonsus M Liguori, CSSR

Treatise on Prayer
by St Alphonsus M Liguori, CSSR

Utopia
by St Thomas More

Vera Sapentia or True Wisdom
Thomas A Kempis

Visits to the Most Holy Sacrament
and the Blessed Virgin Mary
by St Alphonsus M Liguori, CSSR

Vocations Explained
by A Vincentian Father

Where We Got the Bible
by Henry G Graham

New Titles are Being Added Often!

68439887R00085

Made in the USA·
San Bernardino, CA
03 February 2018